THE HERITAGE OF
SCOTLAND
IN COLOUR

THE HERITAGE
OF SCOTLAND

IN COLOUR

A Collection of Forty Colour Photographs

With an Introductory Text
and Notes on the Illustrations by

JOHN KERR

LONDON
B. T. BATSFORD LTD

First published 1956

PRINTED AND BOUND IN THE NETHERLANDS BY L. VAN LEER AND CO. LTD.
AMSTERDAM AND LONDON FOR THE PUBLISHERS
B. T. BATSFORD LTD.,
4 FITZHARDINGE STREET, PORTMAN SQUARE, LONDON, W.I

CONTENTS

LIST OF ILLUSTRATIONS

Cape Wrath
Thurso
Wick
LOCH INCHARD
ISLE OF LEWIS
Stornoway
QUINAG
CANISP & SUILVEN
Lairg
ULLAPOOL
Golspie
LOCH BROOM
LUSKENTYRE SANDS
AN TEALLACH
HARRIS
LOCH MAREE
MACDUFF
Elgin
Dingwall
Peterhead
Nairn
DUNVEGAN CASTLE
Inverness
Portree
SKYE
LOCH DUICH
LOCH NESS
Aberdeen
THE CUILLINS
GLENSHIEL
Dee
Fort Augustus
BALMORAL CASTLE
SANDS OF MORAR
Corpach
Fort William
Montrose
BEN NEVIS
LOCH LEVEN
Forfar
Glen coe
R. ISLA
FALLS OF ORCHY
Dundee
MULL
Perth
Oban
LOCH AWE
DUNDERAVE
ST. MONANCE
LOCH CRAIGNISH
LOCH LOMOND
Kirkcaldy
BASS ROCK
Stirling
JURA
DUNFERMLINE
FORTH BRIDGE
Luss
PRINCES ST.
HOLYROOD
COUROCK
EDINBURGH
SWANSTON
ISLAY
PENTLANDS
Glencorse
KINTYRE
GLASGOW
Clyde
Galashiels
PEAKS OF ARRAN
Tweed
KELSO
Kilmarnock
ST. MARY'S LOCH
Ayr
Teviot
GATESLACK
GIRVAN
Nith

SCOTLAND
showing the places illustrated

Dumfries

0   10   20   30   40   50
MILES

KIRKCUDBRIGHT

MULL OF GALLOWAY

K. C. JORDAN

I   Introducing a Heritage

THE standard works on etiquette advise that in making an introduction a host, or mutual friend, should set new acquaintances off to a good start with a few succinct pointers to their respective backgrounds. Employed with a leavening of commonsense this is an effective social formula. Introducing something on the scale of Scotland and its heritage to an unseen, unknown and mixed audience, however, is a cat of a different colour. From the word go, you are almost certain to find that a good proportion of the patient people at the receiving end of the introduction are already better acquainted with the subject than their host. On the other hand, another section of the audience will probably feel that their host is a pretty dull dog anyway and that their chance of encountering anything of interest through his agency are remote. These are the hazards of introductions which are regrettable but unavoidable.

For the purposes of the succinct pointers which follow, the heritage of Scotland has been confined to a selection of tangible, easy to meet, links with the country's past. Some of the homes of Scottish people, the castles and cottages, which reflect earlier ways of life, and embody native traditions of culture and craftsmanship. The countryside itself, wild and cultivated, has also been included, as the mountains, the glens, and the lower fertile lands are, as it were, the terms of reference within which the nation has developed through the centuries. The fascinating aspect of this heritage is that, in a country so small as Scotland, the various integral features are all intimately associated with each other. All over the country the same influences have been at work. Thomas Telford, for instance, designed the graceful bridge which carries the great north road over the Tay at Dunkeld, he was engaged on the building of the Caledonian canal which links the Firths of Moray and Lorne through Loch Ness and the Great Glen, and he advised the British Fisheries Society on the planning of Ullapool in Wester Ross. In Telford's time, the Governor of the Fisheries Society was the Duke of Argyll who employed Robert Mylne to complete the decoration of Inveraray Castle, and who directed part of the building of the new town of Inveraray at the end of the eighteenth century. Earlier the forbears of the Duke had exerted considerable influence on the castellated architecture of the country by building numerous castles of their own throughout the land from Kilchurn in Loch Awe to Castle Campbell in Dollar Glen, Clackmannanshire, and between times destroying the castles of pretty well everyone else within a far cry of Loch Awe.

Personalities and politics bind all these tangible links into one tightly knit whole, which forms the core of present day Scotland.

In case it should be thought that full justice has not been done to any building, or mountain, or personality, in the ensuing introduction, this should not be attributed to malice aforethought but can safely be put down to ignorance. This then, is a condensed version of personal impressions of Scotland's heritage.

II   Houses Large and Small

TAKE the end of the sixteenth century for a start; at which time the architecture of Scotland began in earnest to shed the mantle of fortification to which it had been thirled for so long. In the north the Burnetts of Leys who had held their lands to the north of the Dee since the time of Robert the Bruce, were building Crathes Castle as a family home. The doubtful political tenor of the close of the century did not encourage any great advance from the traditional lines of a strongly built tower readily adaptable for defence should the need arise. Crathes, therefore, emerged with something of a double personality. From the ground it rises as a very plain tower. The windows, with the exception of later alterations, are small slits easy to shoot from but hard to penetrate from outside. The door is low in a thick wall, and reinforced by a tough wrought-iron grille or "yett", and the corners of the building are rounded to foil attack by battering-ram. So far, little change from the earlier Highland keeps and the peel-towers of the Borders. Above its first three storeys, however, Crathes blossoms out in a great cluster of round and square turrets, and dormer windows supported by highly decorative corbelling. The only warlike feature of this fantasy being a machicolation set in the corbelled base of a window immediately above the door. This incorporates a movable slab of stone providing an aperture from which quicklime or pitch could be poured on the heads of unwelcome callers. As far as the records go there is no evidence of this device ever being used, and it also seems that there was never any occasion for the thick lower walls of the tower to resist any attack. To modern eyes the plainness of the lower portions of the castle make a striking contrast to the exuberance of the detail around its roofline. Various additions have been made to Crathes through the years; to the east a pleasant dignified wing dating from the first half of the eighteenth century and, running north from this, another from the reign of Queen Victoria. The late Sir James Burnett used to enjoy telling the story of a guest who had once looked at the Victorian wing with horror, obviously feeling that it clashed badly with the older building, and asked ,'Who on earth put that up?" Sir James with equal feeling replied "My father." At which, he recalled, his guest allowed his expression to soften and murmured, "Damn good." But, the merits or demerits of the Victorian addition apart the old L-shaped tower in its coat of warm, rose-tinted harling still dominates everything else.

Further to the south, on the Fife shore of the Firth of Forth a much smaller and more domestic house which has also survived the centuries, was in the making at the same time as Crathes. This is the Palace of George Bruce in Culross. Its name has no connection with Royal associations but is simply a variation on the word 'place'—meaning a house or home. While the Burnetts in the north were still slightly preoccupied with the possibilities of war, George Bruce was devoting his wholly civilian energies to making a fortune from the coal seams under the Forth. Having made steps in the right direction he invested some of his profits in what is now considered to be one of the most interesting houses in the country. One range, with its gable to the shore, is dated 1597, and set at right angles to it facing the shore is another wing forming a second side to a courtyard, dated 1611. The house has a wealth of the intriguing detail used in architectural decoration at that time. Its upper storey rooms have dormer windows let into the roof, and the pediments of these have all been embellished with carving. In the interval between building the two wings of the Palace, George Bruce was knighted and the honour is here emblazoned for posterity; the carved date of the earlier portion of the house is accompanied by the initials G.B. and on the later section by the initials S.G.B.

At about this time the population of Edinburgh was beginning to feel the pinch for living room within the confines of the old town on the rock. So they did what was later done on Manhattan Island, New York, and expanded vertically. From an ever increasing demand for accommodation the tall tenements, or 'lands' as they were called, grew up along the sides of the Royal Mile from the Castle to the Palace of Holyrood. Those early burgesses and builders of Edinburgh evolved yet another device for stealing space by introducing an arcade which allowed them to build an extra room's width above the pavement from the first floor up. But even this did not prevent living conditions from being abominably crowded. Probably the plumbing arrangements at Crathes and Culross Palace were as elementary as those in Edinburgh, but the country laird and the small-town industrialist at least had reasonable room to move around in their newly built homes. Their counterparts, the lords, lawyers, judges, and merchants, in Edinburgh, lived in squalor by comparison and these conditions contin-

11

ued well into the eighteenth century. Indeed one of the leading lawyers of the eighteenth century, Campbell of Succoth, had a flat in James's Court off the Lawnmarket where his clerks worked in a cupboard-sized room without heating. When one of his influential clients, such as the Duke of Argyll, came to see him their business was conducted in Campbell's bedroom.

Despite such assorted pre-occupations as guarding against sudden armed attack in the north, extracting under-water coal in Fife, and struggling for space to live in Edinburgh, these men of the sixteenth century found time to introduce some colour into their domestic lives. There has survived in a number of houses throughout the country a fascinating nucleus of interior decoration from this period, in the form of delightfully fresh tempera paintings found on walls and ceilings. In the Chapel of Stobhall, the Scottish home of the Earl of Perth, overlooking a bend in the river Tay between Perth and Blairgowrie, there is a ceiling of rare brilliance. Sparkling likenesses of *Rex Mauritanae*, *Prester John*, *Rex Hungariae*, *Imperator Tvreary*, *Rex Sveviae*, *Rex Hispaniae*, *Rex Magnae Britanniae*, *Rex Poloniae*, *Imperator Germaniae*, and *Rex Galliae* have miraculously retained their colour for more than three centuries, and somehow avoided desecration. There is a rakish touch about the drawing of the figures which suggests that they were painted by a comparatively untrained hand. The figures, all of which are mounted on horseback with the exception of *Rex Mauritanae* who has an elephant, are painted in natural earth colours, and the floral designs of the surrounds and beams are carried out in delicate yellows and greens with outlines of dull red. Above the chapel door the heraldic red and gold of the Drummond family appears on their coat of arms together with the motto, "Gang Warily."

The painted ceiling in the Chapel of the Palace of Falkland in the Kingdom of Fife, as it appears now, is later in date than the Stobhall paintings. Falkland was a hunting palace of the Stuart kings and its chapel was decorated to commemorate the coronation of Charles I as King of Scots in 1633. There are traces of even earlier decoration under this work but these are almost indistinguishable. Blue is a prominent colour in this ceiling which includes Royal badges of the houses of Stuart and Tudor and a pattern of scrollwork in which Charles' monogram, CR for *Carolus Rex* appears with that of his son CP—*Carolus Princeps*, and that of his queen, Henrietta Maria, MR—*Maria Regina*. Over the altar at the eastern end of the chapel the centre panel of a tester is painted in blue and white, the colours of the St. Andrew's Cross. As in the case of Stobhall the painting is not considered to be of high artistic merit, but it is gay and attractive and

12

under it the people of Falkland sit in church as they did three hundred years ago.

Greater attention has been paid to detail in the three excellent tempera paintings at Crathes Castle. These have a formality about them which might indicate a more skilled hand at work. In one room the nine Nobles, or Nine Worthies, of old have been depicted boldly in rich strong pigments. The Nobles and their exploits were the stock in trade of mediaeval minstrels and troubadours who wandered from castle to castle to sing their ballads and provide music for banquets. Hector of Troy, Alexander the Great and Julius Caesar represent the pagan heroes; there are three from the Old Testament, Joshua, David, and Judas Maccabeus; and three Christian heroes—King Arthur, Charlemagne, and Godfrey of Bouillon. In their formal cut and fine colours they look rather like a good hand from a mediaeval pack of playing cards. The beams supporting the ceiling carry black-letter rhymes telling of the heroes' deeds and a final couplet rounds off with the question—"Gude redar tell me or you pass, Whilk of these myn maist valiant was?" Another ceiling in Crathes carries figures of the nine muses, and the five virtues, Wisdom, Justice, Faith, Hope and Charity; and another a miscellany of decorative figures with no connecting theme. All these paintings almost certainly date from about the time when the castle was completed in 1596. At a later date they were covered by lath and plaster and were only brought to light again in the last quarter of the nineteenth century. It was then found that their magnificent colours had hardly been impaired, and indeed the covering up process might have helped to protect and preserve them.

Several other comparable paintings have survived in Guthrie Aisle, in Angus, Gladstone's Land in the Lawnmarket of Edinburgh, Delgaty Castle in Aberdeenshire, and Earlshall and the Palace of Culross in Fife. As yet the study of this tempera work is very much in its infancy, and there is no great amount of reliable information on the history of the paintings, except that in most cases the date has been pretty well established. For some years the pundits have attributed most of this work to itinerant Flemish or German artists, on the grounds that they bear a certain resemblance to paintings of similar date on the continent. It took a visiting art historian from Sweden to gain a hearing for the theory that the paintings were very probably done by native craftsmen. The reasoning being that Scotland has not much of an artistic tradition, and the tempera paintings look more like the work of artisans than artists.

With ceilings as with most other things fashions change. A century and a half after the robust, rough and ready vogue of the tempera painting

13

had seen its heyday Robert Adam was designing his chaste masterpieces in plaster, tinted in soft pastel colours. Adam refined plasterwork to an exquisite degree. The urns which he used as a recurring motif linked by chains of plaster beading, his griffons, his cherubs and his geometrical compositions are all of an impeccable delicacy.

At Mellerstain, for instance, in Berwickshire, the home of the Earl of Haddington there is some of the most outstanding of his interior decoration to be found in Scotland. In the library he built up ornamental cartouches in plaster to frame three medallion oil paintings in the ceiling, and introduced what can only be called a deep frieze, occupying about a third of the depth of the wall to the tops of the bookcases, carrying classical groups of figures in relief. The dining-room ceiling has a circular, plaster centrepiece surrounded by an octagonal garland of floral design which in turn is enclosed by another octagon of more pronounced geometry, and from the ends of the ceiling two half-moon motifs throw their curves in towards the centre. Dark tones in the colouring are used to throw up the extraordinarily fine detail, and quieter shades to cover the larger expanses of undecorated plaster. Here as in his other houses Adam kept his colours completely under control. The subtle range of greens, blues, pinks and biscuit in which he worked seem to blend imperceptibly with each other, with no clash to break up the overall unity of the design.

The true measure of Adam's art in this respect has been brought home within recent years at Mellerstain and at Culzean Castle another of his houses in Ayrshire, where it has been necessary to restore the colour of the ceilings. In the case of Culzean the ceilings had lain under a coat of whitewash for a number of years. Sample patches of this had to be scraped carefully away until the original colours showed through and the whole colour design reconstructed by deduction. The exposed patches had to be matched by new paint and then twentieth-century tradesmen had to adapt themselves to eighteenth-century craftsmanship. Obviously in the circumstances it is difficult to judge how closely Culzean and Mellerstain now are to Adam's original conception. But in both cases an honest attempt was made to recapture the feeling of his work, and as they now stand it could hardly be said that they would not do the old master credit.

The round drawing room at Culzean is warmed by a harmony of pinks on its ceilings, and the long drawing room has its pattern of rectangles and lozenges picked out in softly acquiescing greys and blues. At the core of the castle is the magnificent oval staircase supported by three tiers of handsome columns which demonstrate how effective pure white can be in decoration. The stems of these pillars catch glances of reflected colour from the painted walls of their landings and deflect them into the well of the staircase which is lit from above by a glazed cupola. At least there is no doubt about the original craftsmanship at Culzean Castle being a home product. The refined designs of the castle's ceilings were executed by local tradesmen from the small burgh of Maybole nearby. During the work of restoration when some repairs were required the firm of plasterers who had been employed by Adam were able to undertake the work and to provide from their stores the moulds which had been used when the ceilings were originally put up.

The period between wooden ceilings painted in tempera and the more sophisticated creations of Robert Adam saw a transitionary form of plaster ceiling. This was a bold, richly ornamented type of decoration in which the heavy mouldings were left to speak for themselves without any assistance from colour. At Craigievar, which was completed some thirty years after its neighbour Crathes, there are magnificent specimens of this type of work in the vaulted Great Hall, a small drawing room and the Queen's Bedroom. Here the design follows the normal pattern of chunky ribs of plasterwork dividing the ceiling into panels of various shapes some of which enclose isolated mouldings of their own. In contrast to the lack of similarity found in tempera paintings there are a number of indications that a good deal of this heavy plasterwork sprang from one source. Scattered throughout the country in such houses as Winton in East Lothian, the Binns in West Lothian and Castle Wemyss in Fife, identical details crop up and the over-all designs are much the same. Richly worked plaster pendants as lighting fixtures are features of the Great Hall at Craigievar and the Sea Room at the Binns. Identical moulded medallions of two early Scottish kings, David and Alexander, are also repeated at Craigievar, the Binns and Castle Wemyss which seems to indicate that the plasterers of the early seventeenth century were as keen as the next man to make the fullest use of an attractive detail of decoration once they had taken the trouble to design it. Incidentally, the Binns ceilings were another instance of decoration in preparation for the coming of Charles I in 1633.

During the eighteenth century the last vestiges of the fortified castle were completely supplanted by the mansion-house, with its large windows and its horizontal rather than vertical lay-out. The forerunner of this type of building in Scotland was Kinross House, overlooking the waters of Loch Leven, designed by Sir William Bruce who was responsible for the reconstruction of the Palace of Holyrood. In plan Kinross is a pleasing rectangle. Its facade follows the classical pattern which had already been well established in England. The masonry is all of dressed stone as distinct from the roughly hewn blocks and rubble that went into the older castles, and the angles of its outside wall, far from being "bull-nosed" to fend off battering rams, are decorated with Corinthian pilasters. The facade is flanked by attractive pavilions, one of which leads into the garden. The whole emphasis is calculated towards elegance and beauty, characteristics which were achieved more by accident than design in earlier building.

Hopetoun House near South Queensferry in West Lothian is a mixture of the work of Sir William Bruce and one of his notable successors, William Adam, who was for a time his clerk of works. Bruce finished the original Hopetoun at the very beginning of the eighteenth century, and then about 1721 Adam was employed to make additions. The east front of the house with its pavilions and connecting colonnades was the result of Adam's work, and makes an extraordinarily extended facade. Hardly any of the interiors of the additional building at Hopetoun had been started when Adam died and these were completed by his sons, including Robert, following their father's designs.

An earlier and smaller example of William Adam's architecture is The Drum at Gilmerton, a district of Edinburgh, which still retains its lawns and parklands in spite of an enormous spread of municipal housing schemes on all sides. Surmounting the central section of the front of the house he introduced an innovation in the form of a large pediment. This is probably the first use of such a feature in Scotland. It appears again in more ornate form on the facade of Duff House, formerly a residence of the Earls of Fife, which Adam built on the west bank of the Deveron south of the towns of Banff and Macduff. Here too he used Corinthian pilasters as a decoration in the same way as his old master, Bruce, had done at Kinross House.

The name of Adam is perhaps more closely identified with Robert, William's son, to whose talent and prodigious capacity for work the elegant age of the end of the eighteenth century owed so much of its fine building. After helping to finish his father's designs at Hopetoun, Robert undertook a grand tour in Italy and returned steeped in the classical tradition which is reflected in all his designs. Adam, like all the great architects, had something more to offer than just architecture. He was basically a master designer. He visualised his houses complete; furnished and decorated to the last detail. At Culzean Castle, for instance, the little side tables he designed for the round drawing room have curved backs to fit the sweep of the wall. Here, too, there are delightful examples of candle sconces and wall mirrors which bear the hall-mark of his light touch. Whatever he set out to do he seemed to accomplish with infallible grace. His passion for detail was all-embracing enough to cover the very door knobs. Instead of specifying these fittings from a standard pattern book, he designed them on his drawing board and had them produced by craftsmen, so that they should blend exactly as he wished as part of one grand conception.

His interests indeed actually invaded the sphere of manufacture. He and his family had a long association with Carron Iron Works, the great foundry near Grangemouth on the Forth, once renowned as an ammunition factory and which gave its name to a type of large calibre naval gun called the carronade. Carron also produced the attractive basket grates which Robert Adam designed as centrepieces for his delicately modelled fireplaces. There has been talk in recent years of some of these designs, which are still in the company's files, being revived and brought back into production.

Almost all of Adam's great houses conform to the classical theme around which he devised so many fine variations. One of the exceptions to this generality is the exterior of Culzean Castle which is Adam's own version of the Scottish baronial style. Here he has introduced, in the facade overlooking the gardens, traditional castle features such as round corner turrets and battlements purely as a form of external decoration. On the other side of the house looking out across the Firth of Clyde to the hills of Arran and to Ailsa Craig, a great round tower is the dominant feature of the design. Whether this departure from his usual style was due to the influence of his client, the 10th Earl of Cassillis for whom Culzean was built, or whether inspiration sprang from the impressive and dramatic cliff site, history does not relate. But even when working with castellated features Adam assembled them in the classical manner. Discounting the west wing at Culzean built at the end of the nineteenth century, the symmetry of the castle quickly falls into line with other Adam compositions. And, of course, once inside the castle the use of space and the interior decoration revert entirely to true Adam design. In the formal gardens and the approaches close to the castle the castellated idea is repeated. The terraces between the Parlour Court and the Fountain Court are supported by embattled walls, and the ruinous "gatehouses" at the entrance to the carriageway leading up to the castle were designed as ruins on Adam's original plans. The carriageway itself is in fact an arched viaduct, although only the tops of the arches can now be seen from the Fountain Court. In earlier days the Fountain garden was part of a ravine which almost isolated the castle site from the rest of the policies, and for many years the tenants of the Kennedy's estates were charged to dump loads of litter and rubble into this gorge to make a foundation for the garden.

Culzean has also a rather special domestic interest. The 10th Earl of Cassillis for whom it was built, and who took a considerable detailed

17

interest in the plans, was a bachelor. As a result the building is not nearly as large as one would expect. There are in fact very few rooms in the castle as compared with other country houses of the period. It is obviously sufficient for a bachelor's needs, but with little scope for expansion as a family home. Hence the west wing, which was added at the end of last century when the family found the limited accommodation of the Adam castle too restricted for the Victorian era.

Robert Adam was one of the architects employed in the creation of the New Town of Edinburgh and was in at the very beginning of Princes Street, in both senses of the phrase. The only truly notable building now left among the miscellany of Princes Street is Adam's Register House at the east end, built to house the national historical records of Scotland. It has been altered a good deal since Adam's time but the street front with its proportion, sense of scale, and the details of windows and columns and pediment, and the dome of its central hall rising behind, are all completely Adam in character. Perhaps one explanation of the durability which is another feature of Adam's building is the altruistic outlook of the architect. In the case of Register House he took the trouble to stipulate that no building should be carried out during the winter, and that work done in the summer should proceed at a leisurely pace in order that the various parts of the building might have a proper chance to settle and consolidate. The leisurely pace was maintained for twenty years before the building was completed, and during that time although Adam was in London he kept himself informed on all phases of progress, and kept a controlling hand on the job. By coincidence Culzean took almost the same twenty years to build: like Register House it was completed in 1792 the year of Adam's death. Register House, however, does not have quite the same record of local craftsmanship as Culzean. At least in the early stages of the work on this building Adam suggested that a good "bricklayer" should be brought up from London as he was not impressed by what he had seen of that trade in Edinburgh.

*　　*　　*

The eighteenth century which produced Robert Adam and other architects devoted to art and gracious living, also saw something new in the way of villages and small towns, which was in effect the beginnings of Town and Country Planning. In that era the planner was more often than not the local laird, in some cases assisted by an architect but in others rather making up his own plan as he went along. One of the first of these planned towns was Inveraray at the head of Loch Fyne in Argyll. Here the new plan was conceived and put into practice in about 1742 and is contemporary with the building of the present Inveraray Castle, the home of the Duke of Argyll. Robert Mylne, of the family who had been King's Master Masons for generations, may well have had a hand in the layout of the town as he was employed by the Duke for work on the castle. Certainly the proportions of the houses flanking the broad main street, which slopes very gently up from the loch shore, are delightful. These buildings do not have the same refinements of detail as the little Georgian houses of Kirkcudbright but they have the same basic charm of pleasing shape with the elevations broken up in just the right proportion by windows and doors. They do however adhere to the strong colour tradition which still persists in patches all over the country. The Inveraray houses are, in the main, painted or lime-washed in white, with black used to pick out the window surrounds and down pipes and helping to emphasise the natural grace of the composition of the street as a whole. Occasional houses have a coat of ochre or some other bolder wash. The only evidence of back-sliding is one shop which has its front decorated in a pseudo fish-scale motif to advertise its wares. Down by the shore the Argyll estates office makes a splendidly ducal contribution to the colour scheme with its pulsating strawberry distemper.

The vista of the main street in Inveraray is closed half way by the parish church standing in its own square at the crest of the rise from the loch. Here at the heart of the town the church expresses something of the grander building of the eighteenth century, but is perfectly in keeping as a climax to the smaller domestic houses running from it on either side. Its four corners are supported by simple round columns, and panels of masonry on its two facades, filled in with white lime-wash, contrast with the exposed dressed stone work of the rest of the building. Originally a slender spire rose from the roof of the church to complete its design as the focal point of the town, but this suffered a sad end. As is the way of spires, it began to show structural faults, never really recovering from being struck by lightning in the early nineteenth century, and was eventually taken down for safety's sake. The stones were carefully numbered during the dismantling so that it could be erected again when funds were available. But, during the late war, either in ignorance or in a bout of misplaced zeal, an army unit used the stones for bottoming some military road or other that obviously seemed of utmost importance at the time. The church has two facades, two entrances, and is indeed two churches built under one roof, to accommodate two congregations; one English-speaking and one Gaelic. Further round the head of Loch Fyne past the castle of Dunderave on the Inveraray-Arrochar road the little hexagonal-shaped church of Cairndow again white-washed

19

gives an idea of how the trend of church architecture was beginning to swing only twenty years after the Inveraray church was built.

Fochabers on Speyside in Morayshire has an architectural history very similar to that of Inveraray. Towards the end of the eighteenth century the fourth Duke of Gordon commissioned John Baxter an Edinburgh architect to rebuild Gordon Castle. This project led to the removal of the town from its old site in the immediate vicinity of the castle so that the parklands and policies could be improved. Baxter, therefore, found himself with the additional commission of laying out the new town of Fochabers about a mile to the south. The result is another planned township, this time laid out as a quadrangle with a central square, or *place*, cut back from both sides of the main street. The houses of Fochabers are rather more stylised than those of Inveraray and lack the gaiety of colour wash, but they have a strikingly attractive unity. Again the main street, which is also the main road from Elgin to Banff and Macduff, is broad and airy. And, again, the hub of the plan is a gracefully built parish church dated 1797 set on the south side of the square. This is known as Bellie Kirk and its portico and spire and its lines in general are straight out of the classical Georgian tradition. Like its contemporary at Inveraray, Bellie Kirk has had its tribulations and trials. The 155th anniversary of its building was marked by a proposal for its demolition initiated by a special commission of the Assembly of the Church of Scotland. After a deal of wrangling, negotiating, recrimination, and appealing for funds a group of local parishioners, a son of the Bellie Manse, and a representative cross-section of Scottish notabilities managed to parry this stroke of folly and to secure the safety of the Kirk for the future. Eaglesham in Renfrewshire is another planned village from the end of the eighteenth century. It was founded by the Earl of Eglinton after the older village on the site had been demolished. The Eglinton plan was not actually completed but the village has at least a core based on the enlightened traditions of its period.

Bowmore on the island of Islay, which lies south of Jura, was planned very much on the pattern of Inveraray, and Kenmore in the Breadalbane country of Perthshire was also designed around its church in the late eighteenth century. This period, of course, gave birth to Ullapool under the aegis of the British Fisheries Society, and Macduff was building at the same time at the instigation of the Earl of Fife.

Even earlier, at the very beginning of the eighteenth century, some semblance of a sense of planning was making itself felt in village and small burgh building. In 1689, in which year the mighty Drumlanrig Castle in Dumfriesshire was completed, the little township around the Cathedral of

Dunkeld in Perthshire was destroyed by Jacobite highlanders pressing home their advantage after a victory over the army of William and Mary at the Pass of Killiecrankie nearby. The highland troops besieged the newly formed regiment of Cameronians, under the soldier poet Lt.-Col. William Cleland, in the town but met with such stubborn resistance that they finally set fire to the thatched roofs of the cottages and withdrew leaving them to burn to the ground. It is possible that the present lay-out of Dunkeld, dating from its reconstruction, was based on the plan of the village before the fire.

The High Street breaks off at right angles from the present Great North Road and widens into the Cross making the shape of a rough triangle. From the south end of the base of this triangle a narrow street runs up to the gates of the Cathedral. A considerable number of the houses in these three streets—High Street, the Cross, and Cathedral Street—have survived from the rebuilding of the town. They are plain, unpretentious, coloured in ochre and white-wash, low-built and extremely pleasant in their simplicity. In all probability Cathedral Street, at least, stands on the site of the old canonry where the canons and other churchmen lived when the Cathedral was one of the most powerful churches in the kingdom. As seen now the little houses of old Dunkeld look as if they might have been planned deliberately as a setting for the Cathedral. Their modesty combined with the sudden narrowing of the Cross into Cathedral Street has the effect of emphasising, and perhaps flattering, the handsome soaring lines of the great church. Perhaps the Atholl family, who were principal landowners in the district, had a hand in the planning but it is unlikely that they would have had much to do with the design of the houses. It is probably fair therefore to give the credit for a remarkably appropriate architectural composition to the natural good taste and craftsmanship of the tradesmen who built the town. Other towns like Culross and Crail in Fife which have retained something of their character from times earlier than the rebuilding of Dunkeld do not show the same signs of order. They have, rather, grown up piecemeal with houses built on sites practical and convenient to the needs of the moment. And, of course, they have their own particular charm and the quality of surprise as a result.

Throughout the country these little houses built by artisans without the assistance of any architect keep cropping up to enliven and enhance their surroundings. A mile west along the Tay from Dunkeld is the tiny hamlet of Inver whose chief claim to a mention in any guidebook is that it was the birthplace of Neil Gow the eighteenth-century fiddler whose music so delighted Burns. It also has a very attractive group of buildings set back from a sharp corner in the road similar in character to the houses of

21

Dunkeld. At Inveresk in Midlothian there are some fine houses dating from the eighteenth century, although these are more in the nature of laird's dwellings and do not conform to the normal run of artisan's house. The predecessor of the present church in this village was of great age and had once been given as a present to the church of Dunfermline by Malcolm Canmore. Stirling has a wealth of distinguished domestic building at the top of the town, on the approaches to the Castle, which bears comparison on an equal footing with the Royal Mile of Edinburgh. The list could go on and on but perhaps the point is well enough made. These little houses are to be found all over Scotland, but often they need to be looked for. They do not figure so largely in the tourist itineraries as they might do, and are more likely to be classified as "insanitary slums unfit for human habitation" on account of their age. Despite these irrelevancies however, they are an integral part of the face of Scotland. They are important not only as places of interest and beauty but as the foundations on which the twentieth century rests, and, as such, present generations have an inviolable responsibility towards them.

III   Countryside and Gardens

SCOTS have always enjoyed a special and close attachment to their countryside by courtesy of a generously worded law of trespass. The right to walk where you will provided you do not cause damage has certainly not always been easy to put into practice in the past but in more recent times the weight of public opinion has achieved freedom of access, within the bounds of reason, to pretty well any part of the country to which anyone would want to go. In this respect Scotland is more enlightened than its neighbour in the south where expensive and not noticeably wieldy machinery has been set up to provide the facility of access through the medium of National Parks.

The one exception to the general rule in Scotland is the island of Rum, lying to the south of Skye, where the proprietor positively discourages landing. But that is a very small exception which will no doubt right itself given time, and there are after all thousands upon thousands of acres of compensation elsewhere in the country. All the great mountain ranges are there to be walked and climbed by those of a mind to do so, and they have all something different to offer. The Cairngorms with four summits higher than 4,000 feet lying to the east of the Spey cope with ski-ing at Easter and boundless walking in the summer. From Aviemore the great cleft of the

Lairig Ghru offers an open invitation to take the short cut through to Deeside. As a walk this is not difficult but it is just long enough to present a tempting challenge. It means setting out fairly early in the morning from Coylumbridge, across the Spey from Aviemore, by the track which leads into Rothiemurchus forest. Here the going is more or less level through the woods and an undergrowth of thick heather. After crossing the Cairngorm Club's footbridge the path follows the Druidh burn for a bit and then splits, sending off tracks to Loch Morlich, the Lairig Ghru, and an alternative return to Coylumbridge. From here the Lairig Ghru path begins to gain height and climbs steadily into the high pass that separates Cairngorm and Ben Macdhui on the east from Braeriach and Cairntoul on the west. The pass is rough and littered with boulders for a good part of the way but the gradient is never steep. Looking back from the summit the great sweep of the pass dips down and spreads out over Rothiemurchus opening up a wide view of Speyside. To the south the cliff faces of Cairn Toul rise behind a shoulder of Braeriach. Beyond the summit the river Dee has its source in the Pools of Dee lying in small hollows in the bed of the pass.

The track follows the Dee in its early burn stages through Glen Dee until it comes to a parting of the ways opposite the crags of Devils Point. One path runs south with the burn, and the more usual route for pass walkers bears east round the lower slopes of Carn a Mhaim to join up with the Luibeg and make for Derry Lodge. Once past the lodge, where deer graze peacefully in the grounds, the fun departs and the walk becomes an ordinary plod along a metalled road to the Linn of Dee. All told the distance is something in the region of twenty miles and the height rises from about 750 feet at Coylumbridge to 2,733 feet at the head of the pass.

Cairngorm itself, although one of the highest mountains in Great Britain, is another comparatively easy walk usually tackled from the north by way of Glenmore Lodge on Loch Morlich. The lodge is used as a centre by the Central Council of Physical Recreation which populates the sides of the mountain in summer with dogged bands of small boys who do not know the meaning of "second wind." They scramble up the even slope of Cairngorm hardly even noticing more experienced elders who are brushed aside to fall into their wake. A hill walker is of course a particularly spineless fraction of humanity. Having reached the top of Cairngorm, and having exchanged opinions on the view with anyone else in the vicinity, and having walked around a bit to look down on the cold black waters of Loch Avon, it is unlikely that he will be able to resist the temptation to cross the four miles or so of plateau between him and the summit of Ben Macdhui.

The same insidious compulsion to have another works its magic just as effectively in the mountains of Glencoe. The heights of the Buachaille Etive Mor, the big Shepherd of Etive, have all the appearance of a pleasant day's exercise. Three miles west of Kingshouse Hotel a footbridge across the river Coupall leads to the lower slopes of the mountain and a good scramble up to the summit of Stob Dearg, the peak which looks so impressive when seen from the east. The top of the hill resembles these conceptions of the surface of the moon so familiar to younger generations through the medium of space literature. The rough scattered rocks which give a firm grip to nailed boots are bleached and clean, and look as if they had been born of fierce volcano heat. Beyond the Moor of Rannoch, stretching suddenly flat from the base of the Buachaille, the sharp silhouette of Schiehallion rises away to the east. The immediate prospect is the ridge of the Buachaille Etive Mor running about two and a half miles to the south-west, breaking out into the peaks of Stob na Doire, Stob Coire Altruim, and Stob na Broige on the way. To climb the Buachaille and walk the ridge is really quite a fair day's sport, taking into account the return journey. But arrival at Stob na Broige produces a positive vertigo of temptation to plunge down one smooth flank of the Lairig Gartain, losing 1,500 precious feet, and swing up the other to gain the neighbouring ridge of the Buachaille Etive Beag, the little Shepherd of Etive.

Ben Lawers on the north shore of Loch Tay in Perthshire, a near neighbour of Schiehallion, is a very different kind of mountain. It is only sixteen feet short of the 4,000 foot mark but like Ben Nevis and Cairngorm does not give the immediate impression of being a very high mountain, because of its contours. Its slopes are completely grass covered and provide something for the sheep to nibble right up to the summit. By a purely coincidental combination of geology, altitude and climate Ben Lawers has achieved renown for the wealth of arctic-alpine flowers to be found on its slopes. The Ben Lawers-Caenlochan schist, which also occurs at the head of Glenisla, provides the basic salts of calcium, magnesium, potassium, sodium and iron on which this rich flora thrives. There is, too, good snow cover in the winter months, which helps to ensure the survival of these tiny plants, and the height gives continuity of low temperatures during the other seasons. On the lower reaches of the mountain, meadow flowers such as the alpine lady's mantle, *Alchemilla alpina*, and a number of varieties of the orchis family grow in profusion. Higher up, great pink cushions of the moss campion, *Silene acaulis*, are not too hard to find, and the yellow mountain saxifrage, *Saxifraga aizoides*, droops in clumps over the banks of little mountain streams. It is, however, the moist ledges inaccessible to sheep where the wonderful colour of the flowers of Lawers is to be seen in concentration. From a distance of say ten yards the steep faces overlooking Loch na Chat appear to be nothing more than rock breaking through tufts of green grass and moss. In close-up they can reveal brilliant natural rock gardens. Rose-root, *Sedum rosea*, with its grey-green succulent leaves and yellow flowers, and the rich, blue alpine forget-me-not, *Myosotis alpestris*, keep company with "tall herbs" such as the elegant globe flower, *Trollius europaeus*, which balances its bright yellow head, almost as large as a ping-pong ball, on a slender stalk. Protected by a thick blanket of snow in the winter and nurtured by the natural resources of the rock and water of the mountain these rare and beautiful flowers bloom annually into a surprise of colour in June and July, as they have done since the ice-age.

*   *   *

Although there were gardens in Scotland in the sixteenth and seventeenth centuries they were few and far between and tended towards the practical rather than the decorative. In general the emphasis on defence in larger houses precluded the luxury of a garden and there is also reasonable evidence that no great store was set by attractive surroundings. Even as late as the early eighteenth century plantations of shelter trees around houses were not common except perhaps in the Lothians, and where there were trees they tended to be so hard up against the building that they shut out air and light. When the ordinary garden did come into being it was apt to be scattered hugger-mugger somewhere in the region of the house and poorly kept. The flowers that were grown now sound unfamiliar and almost Shakespearean; columbine and virgin's bower, throatwort, wall-pellitory, and bear's-ears. Growing alongside these were the popular herbs, penny-royal, sweet basil, fennel, hyssop, hore-hound, and celandine, which were used for cooking and as medicine.

The earliest garden to survive in Scotland, as we think of gardens to-day, is the remarkable walled garden of Edzell in Angus laid out by Sir David Lindsay in about 1604. It is a fascinating sidelight of heredity that continuously over five centuries the Lindsay family in Scotland has held a premier place in the realms of art, literature and cultural thought in general. Sir David Lindsay's conception at Edzell was almost a century ahead of its time. There is no record of what was grown in this garden originally, but the richly sculptured walls remain as some indication of the grandeur that must once have been. Within these walls the garden, now under the care of the Ministry of Works, has been laid out in a formal pattern of flower beds with decorative box-wood borders. The gardens of

Kinross House on Loch Leven, and Pitmedden in Aberdeenshire, both dating from the end of the seventeenth century are others of which only the walls are original. When Kinross House lay empty during the greater part of last century the garden was used annually as a site for the local horse show. It has been revived, however, within the past fifty years and now makes an immaculate setting for the dignity of Sir William Bruce's architecture. Stretching from the house almost to the shore of the loch, the lawn is broken into two levels and divided by rectangular patterns of yew hedges. On the upper lawn the hedges enclose rose beds, and along one of the walls there are great bays of herbaceous plants which give a wonderful show of colour. The whole layout of the garden and the house has been focussed on the ruined tower of Loch Leven Castle on its island out in the loch. The gate in the lochside wall, the central garden path, the two doors of the house, the main drive through the sweep of parks on the approach, and the entrance gates off the main street of Kinross, are all in a direct line with the castle.

At Crathes Castle on Deeside the massive, trimmed yew hedges date from 1702, since when the garden has been established as one of the finest formal lay-outs in Scotland. The hedges and paths and borders cut the garden into several segments each with a definite character of its own. In the Upper Pool garden there is a colour scheme of red and yellow blooms against a purple foliage. Adjoining this, across one of the great banks of yew hedge a mass of blue annuals surround a central fountain, looking like a patch of soft rising mist in the late evening. The June Border, carefully planted to come into flower in the month from which it takes its name, runs from a dovecote in the corner of the garden to meet the White Border in the shade of an old Portugal laurel set at the junction of four turf paths. Between the Camel Garden and the Trough Garden a double herbaceous border displays burning golds, yellows and reds as a glorious foreground for the castle. Every year planting is planned to produce a highlight in some part of the garden at any given time during the summer.

These gardens just mentioned are all situated in the east, or central Scotland; a fact which redounds considerably to the credit of the gardeners concerned for the east lacks the one great advantage of the west coast—the Gulf Stream. This current of warm water out in the Atlantic not only makes the British Isles habitable but creates a climate in the west temperate enough to accommodate exotic flowers and shrubs from the sub-tropics and make them feel at home. Its influence is as effective in the Western Highlands as it is in Cornwall. From Inverewe, a miraculous oasis of colour among the barren mountains of Wester Ross, to Lochinch by the Rhinns of Galloway, the west coast is bespattered with pockets of luxurious rhododendron and azalea bloom throughout the months of May and June. Glenarn at Rhu, in the mouth of the Gareloch on the Firth of Clyde, has one of the finest collections of rhododendrons in Scotland including plants grown from some of the first seed brought into the country. Midway down the west shore of Loch Fyne in the woodland garden of Crarae rhododendrons and azaleas with other shrubs are massed against a background of rare trees. Achamore on Gigha, and Kiloran on Colonsay, have the same wonderul colour to show in their own distinctive settings. At Culzean Castle in Ayrshire there are camellias and magnolias to add to the others, and at Blairquhan not far away on the Girvan water great banks of *Rhododendron ponticum* make a solid hedge of purple bloom along the roadside. It is surprising, is it not, that Scotland should be so popularly accepted as a country of dull greens and browns?

IV   Preserving a Heritage

IT is a sombre fact that a great deal of what must be classified as essential heritage material in Scotland has only very slender hopes for continued survival in the future. This applies particularly to the small houses of the seventeenth, eighteenth and early nineteenth centuries which have no great claim to fame but which contribute so much in the way of simple character and charm to their surroundings. The larger houses, with more pronounced historical and architectural backgrounds, are not so urgently in danger of disappearing. There are many reasons, but few valid excuses, for things having come to such a sorry pass. Probably the main enemy in this minor war of attrition is a powerful atmosphere of apathy, finding its strength in weakness, which almost defies, but not quite, the advances of enthusiasm. It is strange, but true that the vast majority of honest, hardworking, intelligent citizens take little or no interest in the buildings among which they live. They go about their lawful occasions, seldom raising their eyes above shop-window level, or above the ribbon of tarmacadam in front of their cars. As a result the faculty of critical appreciation has plumbed new depths in this twentieth century and can be assumed to be languishing somewhere near the bottom of the barrel. To substantiate such a sweeping generality is painfully simple. You need only look at any average housing scheme erected within the past thirty years to find dreich and drab design unalleviated by anything in the way of colour; rows upon rows of deathly grey rough-cast walls without a shape or a feature to call their own. If that is not

27

enough, have a look at any average specimen of bungaloid growth where you will find every bizarre shape that the human mind can conceive, plus a few that just happened, and wall after wall adorned in Dorset pea pebble-dash. If people did look at architecture and realised the significance of what they saw such wonders of mediocrity would cease forthwith.

What is perhaps more important is that this apathy cuts two ways. Not only does the bad pass uncriticised, but good, old building is also unnoticed and suffers neglect accordingly. In the thirty years during which so much of the former has been erected higgledy-piggledy around the country, a sad amount of the latter has been allowed to decay beyond repair, or has been deliberately demolished. There seems to be a fetish in official circles, where power rests, that an old house is an uneconomic problem, and something to be got rid of quickly before it gives trouble. The specious arguments produced to justify action on those lines usually include a carefully prepared list of defects—the house is damp, it has no bathroom, the ceiling heights do not conform to modern standards, and the windows are too small. It would be refreshing to hear of a burgh surveyor's report on an old property which indicated that he thought something could be done to cure damp, that he did not consider the addition of a bathroom insurmountable, that in view of the fact that the house was in the country he felt regulations concerning ceiling heights and window space might be stretched a little, and that he thought a restoration of this kind could be achieved for a good deal less than the cost of demolishing the house and building anew.

It is unfair to suggest that the present unsatisfactory state of affairs can be laid entirely at the doors of the poor old general public, and local authorities. The professionals, architects and planners, have also been sadly lacking in initiative and perception. If trained brains such as theirs can do no better than they have done, it is rather hard to blame the layman for his shortcomings. Surprising as it may seem neither of the colleges of architecture in Glasgow or Edinburgh give the traditional domestic building of Scotland a place in their courses of instruction. Their alumni are launched into the hard world of professional practice with only the glimmerings of a feeling for the older buildings among which they must be expected to work. A few rise above their education and find out for themselves, the majority stay under and Scotland is the poorer for it.

This should not be taken as the manifesto of a heels-in-the-ground traditionalist to whom all that is old is good, and all that is new, insufferable. It is rather the view of a congenital supporter of the under-dog, and asks only that the old should be given a fair deal. There is obviously great scope for new building in Scotland, as elsewhere, in which modern design and techniques should be developed and encouraged. But this should not mean a total submersion of the old. So often in this connection it appears that planning begins at the wrong end. Say, for example, that a county planning committee has within its area of administration a small town or village generally recognised as of outstanding architectural interest. It would be not only reasonable but sensible to assume that the notable architecture should be the focal point of any development plan for the future. But taking an average of the recent history of planning in Scotland the more probable outcome would be a new conception of shopping centres, bus stations, and road widening schemes, qualified with a pious expression of regret, "that it had been found unavoidable to cope with the increasing needs for improvement, based on estimated population densities, without reluctantly having to sacrifice some of the attractive examples of early architecture for which the town is renowned throughout Scotland." In this way, and by other less tortuous devices, considerable devastation has already been worked upon the little houses of Scotland. It is therefore all the more important that those which have survived, should be cherished, and that their merits should be appreciated and weighed in the balance, or the face of Scotland will lose an irreplaceable facet of its enchantment.

Index

Loch Craignish

On the west coast the mainland of Scotland is held together by innumerable slender threads of land which have so far resisted the eroding advances of the Atlantic. Loch Craignish in Argyll only retains its identity by courtesy of the narrow peninsula which protects its north-western shore. Without this the loch would be no more than the anonymous end of the Sound of Jura. Towards the end of the peninsula the comparatively modern mansion house of Craignish Castle occupies the austere site of its predecessor, a fifteenth-century keep where the Campbells of mediaeval times kept their own company. At the mouth of the loch a fast-running tide-race cuts its way between the cliffs of Craignish Point and their opposite numbers on the little island of Garbhreisa forming a strait by the name of Dorusmore, the great door. Inland at the head of the loch the waters are deep and calm and all that a good anchorage should be. The road from Oban to Lochgilphead climbs the high ground to the east of the loch. From here the dark rocks and a liberal sprinkling of green, wooded islands, some of which still respond to crofting, add contrast to the rippling sheen of the water. Beyond, the demure shape of Scarba rises from the sea, cut off from the Jura by the gulf and whirlpool of Corryvreckan. Through the gulf it is possible to glimpse the fertile little island of Colonsay which takes its name from St. Columba. To the south-west the generous decolletage of the Paps of Jura—Beinn-an-Oir, mountain of gold; Beinn Diuntaidh, hallowed mountain; and Beinn-a-Chaolais, mountain of the Firth—pops distinctively into the view, and to the north-west over Arduaine and the Firth of Lorne the mountains of Mull loom more sombrely.

Photo: Fred G. Sykes

Loch Awe

The normal order of highland scenery is reversed in the case of Loch Awe. Its head, about three miles east of Craignish, is comparatively tame and its foot provides a grand climax in the massif of Ben Cruachan. This anomaly is probably due to an earth tremor which changed the scene of things by cracking open the Pass of Brander along the base of Cruachan so allowing the loch to flow unnaturally north-west to meet Loch Etive. The dark ravine of the Pass suggests the violence of earthquake and there is a feeling, when driving through, that the river is escaping turbulently in the wrong direction. From the road, by Loch Awe railway station, under the south-east shoulder of Cruachan the view takes in the ruins of Kilchurn Castle, built in the fifteenth century by Sir Colin Campbell of Glenorchy, the Black Knight of Rhodes, who was the founder of the Breadalbane family. Close to the castle the river Orchy enters the loch and, behind, the distinctive ridge of Ben Lui, the mountain of the fawns, rises to its summit of 3708 feet. From the slopes of Ben Lui four burns run to feed four of the great lochs of the highlands: Loch Tay to the east, Loch Awe to the west, and Loch Fyne and Loch Lomond to the south. This part of Argyll has been Campbell country for hundreds of years. Its remoteness and the restricted approaches gave rise to the clan's old war cry, "It's a far cry to Lochow," a nobler and more confident variant of the small boy's challenge, you'll no' catch me. Today, the Duke of Argyll, chief of Clan Campbell, lives at Inveraray Castle at the head of Loch Fyne, the inland neighbour of Loch Awe.

Photo: J. Allan Cash

The Falls of Orchy

The Orchy is a river of Argyll which starts out under the name of the water of Tulla within a few miles of the Perthshire boundary. To the south of its upper reaches stands a fragment of Achallader Castle, built in the early seventeenth century by Black Duncan Campbell, a descendant of the builder of Kilchurn on Loch Awe. After being crossed by the main road between Tyndrum and Glencoe the river expands into Loch Tulla, fringed with pine trees and overlooked by the bowl of Stob Ghabhar. The loch collects several tributaries from the Black Mount, one of the finest sporting estates in Scotland, and narrows at its foot to discharge the Orchy proper. It is from here, through the green and rocky Glenorchy, to its meeting with the Lochy coming in from the east that the river offers some of its best fishing. In a series of sparkling, gurgling runs, punctuated by quieter pools where the salmon and sea-trout take their rest between surges upstream, it follows the windings of the lonely glen. About half way through, its gurgle rises to a rumble as the waters break over the buttress of the falls. Turning west with the flow of the Lochy at the end of the glen the river loses its speed in the flat strath-lands. At Dalmally it is divided by a small islet in mid-stream on which Glenorchy parish church was built in 1811. A mile or so further west it picks up the Strae from the neighbouring glen and with it pours into the foot of Loch Awe.

Photo: Fred G. Sykes

Dunderave, Loch Fyne

This is one of the lesser known, small castles of the Highlands, and one of the few to survive the troubles of its time
in a reasonable state of preservation. It has a particular
architectural interest because it shows that the Scottish
style of building had penetrated to the wilds of Argyll
in the sixteenth century. Dunderave, pronounced
Dunderawe, was built by the chief of the Macnaughton
clan on a pleasant little promontory leading off the north-
west shore of Loch Fyne between Inveraray and the head
of the loch. Originally the Macnaughtons had held lands
on the shores of Loch Awe, as neighbours of the
Campbells, with an ancient fortress on the tiny island of
Fraoch Eilean near Kilchurn. A carved lintel above the
door of Dunderave bears the date 1596 together with an
inscription and the motto of the clan, "I hope in God."
One architectural concession to the uncertainty of highland life in the late sixteenth century was the round tower
built into the corner of the castle to the right of this photograph. This is a departure from the traditional L-plan to
which the building otherwise conforms, and as it is well
pierced with shot holes it was probably intended purely as
a modified form of fortification. The rest of the house has
its full complement of the features which were in fashion
when it was built—the plain gable with crow-steps leading
up to the chimney, little dormer windows rising out of the
eaves, and on the far side another gable embellished with
round corner turrets. Sir Robert Lorimer, the notable
architect, restored the castle in 1912 after it had lain without a roof for a number of years, and more recently a
simple courtyard garden has been developed.

Photo: G. Douglas Bolton

Loch Lomond at Luss

Loch Lomond is the largest fresh-water loch in Scotland and it has a reputation for natural beauty to match. Admittedly Dr. Johnson had some sour comments to make after journeying along Lochlomondside, and Wordsworth expressed the curious opinion that "a speedier termination of the long vista of blank water" would improve the view, but by and large the reputation has held its own. Perhaps the combination of the loch with the magnificent profile of Ben Lomond, seen in this photograph across the little bay of Luss, is the most impressive scenic feature. At this end, too, the loch is studded with more than twenty islands whose trees and underbrush stand out green against the water. The road leading north winds with the vagaries of the wooded loch shore past Glen Douglas, which is an inviting walk through the hills to Loch Long, to join the Inveraray road near Arrochar. At this point a level of less than forty feet separates the fresh water of Loch Lomond from the sea water of Loch Long. Behind Arrochar the craggy outline of the Cobbler, in which some eyes see the outline of the shoemaker at his last, rises boldly, and to the north the greater height of Ben Vorlich marks the head of the loch. It has been said that the loch took its name from the Ben sometime in the thirteenth century and prior to that had been called Leven, which is still the name of the river that runs from it into the Clyde at Dumbarton. Leven is also the root of the district name Lennox which some traditionalists would like to substitute for the more workaday Dunbartonshire. For all its considerable extent Lochlomondside is frequently embarrassed by the vast fleets of tourist traffic which take to the shore road. It is to be hoped that its beauty will not be its undoing.

Photo: Fred G. Sykes

Gourock and the Clyde Estuary

The pier on Kempock Point at Gourock is as near as need be the dividing line on the Clyde, where heavy industry ends and the fun begins. Greenock, its immediate neighbour up river, is busy with sea-going trade, shipyards and engineering works. Two miles to the south-west at Cloch Point the river starts to widen into the firth and a string of holiday resorts stretches down its coastline from Wemyss Bay past Fairlie, where the steamers leave for Arran and the Mull of Kintyre, to Girvan in the south of Ayrshire. Across the estuary from Gourock, in the mouth of the Gareloch, sits Helensburgh whose provost in the memorable year of 1812 launched upon the Clyde its first passenger steamer. The descendants of this three horse-power wonder have established themselves as a sort of folk tradition on the river. Plying from Gourock throughout the summer the Clyde steamers carry thousands of trippers "doon the watter": the old and the young, resplendent in cotton prints, flannels and shirt-sleeves, and funny hats; some of the very young firmly glued to sticks of peppermint rock; and every one prepared to extract the last ounce of unbuttoned enjoyment from the fresh air, the view and the refreshment rooms. The estuary is also a playground for the yachts and small sailing dinghies whose owners match design and skill in summer regattas. Gourock proper looks north over the river to Rosneath, associated with St. Medan of the sixth century and the healing waters of his well, and beyond to the hills of Lochlomondside. From Ashton, the west end of the town, the Hills of Cowal rise into the view behind Dunoon and the Holy Loch.

Photo: G. Douglas Bolton

Even when faced with a handsome view of the hills of Arran across Kilbrannan Sound from the west, it is irresistible to assert that the finest thing on this island is the garden of Brodick Castle which lies beyond these hills on its east coast. In spring and early summer the wooded slopes below the great red sandstone pile blaze with colour. The delicate creamy lemon of the clustered trumpets of *sinogrande*, the largest of the rhododendrons, contrasts with the pinks and rich reds of other species, and in one corner banks of massed azaleas produce a riot of scarlets, oranges and yellows, like a small concentration of the New England fall. The southern slope of Goatfell, the island's highest peak, rises gradually from the woods behind the garden making an easy ascent to the summit. A saddle between Glen Sannox and Glen Rosa connects Goatfell with the crest of Cir Mhor to the west, a string of hills which provides some of the most thrilling ridge-walking in the country. It is these two groups which form the central feature in the view of the northern half of the island from Kintyre. Ben Bharrain to the left is a hill of gentler contours. To the south the island takes on the character of a lumpy plateau enlivened by cliffs round the coastline, but otherwise notable only for the views of the mountains in the north. The whole of Arran has been a property of the Hamilton family since the Earldom of Arran was bestowed on them in the early sixteenth century. Earlier in history Robert the Bruce had raised his standard here and prepared for the assault on the mainland which led to the overthrow of the English, and his coronation as King of Scots. One final geographical digression—the sunset over the peaks of Arran as seen from the Ayrshire coast is a phenomenon of great beauty.

Photo: G. Douglas Bolton

Girvan Harbour

There is a peculiarly statistical interest about the fresh water content of the small harbour at Girvan. This has its source, as the water of Girvan, at a height of some 2050 feet fourteen miles west of the town. By flowing north-west and then south-west it manages to cover thirty-six miles in all before reaching the harbour and passing on into the Firth of Clyde. In the course of its travels it cuts through five lochs, touches six parishes, and offers the hospitality of its banks to five castles and houses of architectural or antiquarian significance—Bargany, Blairquhan, Cloncaird, Dalquharran, and Killochan. This is not counting Kilkerran which is within a salmon cast of the river for anyone who cares to stretch a metaphor. Of these houses at least Bargany and Blairquhan have magnificent gardens to add to the attraction of the moving water, and in the case of Bargany the garden was recorded as "very pretty" as early as the end of the seventeenth century. The standard of building declines with the arrival of the river at Girvan, a town which has seen the rise and fall of the handloom weaving craft and the fishing industry but little movement of consequence in architecture. Stretching away from the harbour there is a fine sand beach which has helped to establish the town's reputation as a coast resort, rather quieter in nature than its northerly neighbours Ayr, Prestwick and Troon. The Saugh hill rises directly behind the town and to the south is its small neighbour the Byne hill, with easy-going walks, and good bramble picking in the season. And, directly opposite the harbour mouth Ailsa Craig lifts its symmetrical bulk of pale grey, curling-stone granite out of the Firth.

Photo: G. Douglas Bolton

Mull of Galloway

Even in these enlightened days of family cars and touring coaches, with "tourism" weighing heavily upon the national conscience, Galloway remains to an astonishing degree off the beaten track. This region, which takes its attractive name from its early inhabitants the Celtic Gauls, includes the two south-western counties of Wigtownshire and the Stewartry of Kirkcudbright. It has fascinating historical associations, delightful hill and loch scenery, and a population aching to welcome visitors, but somehow it has never overcome the handicap of being by-passed by main roads. To the extreme south-west the peninsula of the Rhinns of Galloway is further isolated by the incursions of Luce Bay from the Solway Firth and Loch Ryan from the Firth of Clyde. From the very end of the peninsula the Mull of Galloway thrusts its rocky headland into the Solway to make the most southerly point of the Scottish mainland. Its cliffs rise a good 200 feet sheer from the water and near its tip the white column of the lighthouse adds its own trim contribution to the skyline. The Mull lies on a par with Belfast Lough across the North Channel, and given fair visibility the outline of Ireland can be seen shimmering in the west. Over the broad sweep of Luce Bay the hills of Kircudbright appear in the north-east and due south the Isle of Man breaks into the horizon. Traces of ancient earthworks, thought to be Scandinavian in origin, remain on the Mull and, near the point where it joins with the main peninsula, part of St. Medan's Cave and chapel built into the base of the cliffs has been preserved. The Mull also has its place in legend as the last resort of the Picts. Stepping bravely in where history fears to tread legend gives a lively description of these shadowy people even down to their feet, which were so broad that when it rained they could turn them up and use them for umbrellas.

Kirkcudbright Harbour

A distinguished Dean of the Faculty of Advocates, now elevated to the bench, once remarked in the course of a development-plan enquiry that the native character of Scotland stood in danger of being submerged. If, he said, the popular policy of new houses for old was pursued without check it would soon be difficult to tell whether one was in Hull, Hell, Halifax or Haddington. The first stretch of Kirkcudbright seen on the way in from Castle Douglas is a drab example of the Dean's dilemma. But beyond this the local tradition of paint and colour-wash in exterior decoration irrepressibly asserts itself. Clean greys and blues light up the facades of small Georgian houses, with details of window surrounds, fanlights, doorways and corner stones picked out in contrasting colours. The older and plainer houses sparkle in white lime-wash. A fresh coat is a standard part of the annual ritual of spring cleaning. In the case of Gable-End Cottage which just appears on the extreme left of this photograph the fashion was commendably carried beyond the bounds of logic. For more than fifteen years the cottage stood empty under the vague prospect of demolition, but its owners continued to pay it the courtesy of an annual lime-wash along with the neighbouring Shore Cottage and the large grain store behind. This little clutch of buildings, with its pleasant setting and proportions, has come to be known as the Harbour Group and has been recorded in generations of sketches and water-colours. Seen from the opposite bank of the Dee the towering remains of Maclellan Castle in the heart of the town loom up as an impressive sixteenth-century background. When the long-standing threat to demolish Gable-End Cottage matured into an active proposal the people of Kirkcudbright launched an appeal for a restoration fund, and ensured that the group will remain intact.

Photo: Fred G. Sykes

Colour turning in a clump of shelter trees, a low sun, an empty road, and smooth, rolling hills in the background combine to suggest autumn in the border country. The land looks as if a season's work might have been done, and everything cleared away for the winter. It seems remote, and away from it all, and as if the hills might keep rolling indefinitely. But seclusion in Scotland is a very relative quality. Climb the Aonach Eagach in Glencoe on an unpromising day and you will find for a certainty a companion in folly on the ridge. Go fishing on the Orchy and find yourself in the foreground of a photograph. Or cast around within a radius of roughly five miles from Gateslack and find a hatful of contrasts to set against your starting point. To the south-west, for example, the great soaring block of Drumlanrig, home of the Duke of Buccleuch, dominates the view among its parklands above the Vale of Nith. A tremendous piece of architecture by an unknown hand, but often attributed to Sir William Bruce who reconstructed Holyrood Palace. It was built for the first Duke of Queensberry, now a Buccleuch title, and is said to have ruined him. Well within the cast to the north-east is the delightful little seventeenth-century church of Durisdeer which includes the ornately sculptured tomb of the second Duke of Queensberry. To the south a remnant of the ancient Morton Castle thought to have been founded in the time of Malcolm Canmore. And, flanking the Dalveen Pass are part of Roman earthworks called the Devil's Dyke. All of which helps to demonstrate how tight a little kingdom Scotland can be, in autumn, near Gateslack.

Photo: Fred G. Sykes

St. Mary's Loch

Deep in the hills of Selkirkshire, of which James Hogg the Ettrick Shepherd so sweetly sang, lies the dog-leg of St. Mary's Loch. At its head there is a monument to the poet's memory, and near its foot is the farm of Altrive which he leased on a nominal rent from the Duke of Buccleuch, for the last twenty years of his life. On all sides the grass-covered hills slope down to meet their reflections in the still blue water. Between the head of the loch and its small neighbour the Loch of Lowes, on a narrow neck of low-lying ground, stands Tibbie Shiels Inn where Hogg and his literary friends used to foregather. In earlier days the forest of Ettrick was a stronghold of the free-booters who went cattle raiding over the border, and nearer home when the spirit moved them. Around St. Mary's Loch there are traces of a number of the simply designed but powerfully built peel-towers which these border reivers called home. Up the Megget Water from the crook of the loch's dog-leg is the site of the castle of Piers Cockburn, whose career ended in an Edinburgh execution, by command of James V. Just north of the loch's foot stands Dryhope Tower the home of a sixteenth-century beauty Mary Scott, the Flower of Yarrow. The tower has now passed from Scott hands, but Harden in Roxburghshire, from where Wat Scott came to marry the Flower of Yarrow, has remained in the Scott family, now represented by Lord Polwarth. To the east a little from Dryhope is Mountbenger, another farm worked by the Ettrick Shepherd and one piece of the Forest's landscape on which the farmer in him spoke more loudly than the poet: "A gey cauld place, staunin' yonder on a knowe in a funnel, in the thoroughfare of a perpetual sugh."

Photo: Fred G. Sykes

Kelso Abbey

The four great border abbeys of Jedburgh, Kelso, Melrose and Dryburgh all date from the first half of the twelfth century; with the exception of Dryburgh they were founded by David I; they were all sacked by the Earl of Hertford during his Scottish expedition in the mid-sixteenth century; sacked again with the coming of the Reformation; and now they are all in the care of the Ancient Monuments Department of the Ministry of Works. Kelso ranks second to Jedburgh in date and in some respects is considered to be the most interesting of the group. The original religious order of the Abbey was a group of Tironensian monks moved by David I from his Selkirk estate in 1126. From then until its later misfortunes Kelso grew and flourished under generous royal patronage. Its abbots served frequently as ambassadors and special commissioners of the royal court, and were the first churchmen to appear on the roll of Parliament, with precedence over all other abbots of the kingdom. The last abbot to hold office was James Stuart, a bastard son of James V, whose appointment was concerned more with the revenue derived from church lands than the direction of ecclesiastical affairs. For a time in more recent years it was thought that the tower and other surviving fragments were the remains of a comparatively small abbey church. But investigations based on material in the Vatican Library indicated that the ruins represent only a fraction of what was probably the largest of the border abbeys, and indeed unique in Scotland by virtue of a plan which included a western as well as an eastern transept. The abbey and its lands came into the possession of the Duke of Roxburghe's ancestors after the Reformation and remained private property until placed under the guardianship of the Ministry of Works.

Photo: A. F. Kersting

Bass Rock

To geologists the Bass Rock is an igneous intrusion, or lump of lava, related to the castle rocks of Stirling and Edinburgh, the Abbey Craig on which Wallace's Monument stands above Causewayhead, and Dumbarton Rock in the Clyde. To golfers at North Berwick it is a satisfactorily impassive spectator when a putt lips the hole and stays out on the third green. To ornithologists it is the great breeding ground for gannets in Scotland; and for the keepers who man the lighthouse, the regular visits of bird-watching expeditions make it one of the more sociable outposts of their service. There may be something about volcanic rock which lends itself to violence and derring-do even after it has cooled off. At any rate the Bass has had a surprisingly active career for such a comparatively small intrusion. Its recorded history starts off decorously enough in the eighth century when St. Baldred used the rock as a private retreat. But, towards the end of the seventeenth century, it was bought by the Government and used as a state prison for the Covenanters. Later on the Bass, by one of the pawkiest of military manœuvres, achieved the distinction of being the last bastion to hold out for King James VII. Four young Jacobite officers being held prisoner in the fort somehow managed to close the gates when its entire garrison of some fifty troops was outside unloading a supply boat. When news of this coup leaked out, Jacobite reinforcements landed on the rock, and the French government supplied provisions, ammunition, and two large boats which were used for raiding the coasts of Fife and East Lothian. In all it took three years to starve out the tiny garrison by blockade, and then the terms of surrender included complete freedom.

Photo: J. Allan Cash

Holyrood

The Royal Palaces of Scotland, where the fortunes of the sixteenth century Stuarts fluctuated between gaiety and tragedy, suffered a decline following the departure of James VI for London. This is not surprising when it is recalled that after a visit by Charles II in 1651 no sovereign set foot in Scotland until 1822. Holyrood however had a slightly better time of it than the others. The original palace which had been built by James IV and enlarged by his son had, like their palace at Falkland in Fife, its "lyon's den" where the royal mascot, which travelled with the court, was housed when the king was in residence. Early in the reign of Mary Queen of Scots the palace was destroyed by the English, and then its successor was accidentally burned to the ground when occupied by Cromwell's troops; the Cromwellians, as it happened, were also rather careless at Falkland and brought down the north range there in an accidental fire. Most of the present Holyrood was designed by Sir William Bruce for Charles II, and built by Robert Mylne the King's Master Mason. Although Charles was never to see the palace, he personally approved the plans and had comments to offer on such details as the position of the fireplaces and the width of the entrance gateway. Very little of any of the older buildings has survived, and it is likely that most of the original furnishings followed James VI south. More than 140 years passed between the completion of the building and a visit by a royal court. It was not until the time of Queen Victoria that the palace came into its own again as a royal residence. Since then there have been regular court presentations, and garden parties on the palace lawns with the green and gold uniforms of the Royal Company of Archers, the Queen's Bodyguard in Scotland, to suggest a hint of mediaeval pageantry.

Photo: A. F. Kersting

Princes Street

About 180 years before this picture was taken an Edinburgh merchant was allowed freedom from rates and taxes to encourage him to build the first house in Princes Street. There was some reluctance among the good citizens of that time to leave the canyon of tenements which plunged down the Lawnmarket, High Street and Canongate, on the crest of the ridge from the Castle to the Palace of Holyrood, for the New Town. Nowadays, such is the turn of the screw, high rents and valuations drive merchants reluctantly from this broad mile to less expensive situations. The street has come a long way from its dirt track days when it went by the name of the Lang Gaitt. At the foot of the Mound leading up to the old town, and opposite the opening of Hanover Street, W. H. Playfair built the Royal Institute, now the Royal Scottish Academy with a massive statue of Queen Victoria enthroned on its portico, and later his National Gallery went up on a site just behind. An enormous "mercat cross" erected to the memory of Sir Walter Scott, a few years earlier than the gallery, has survived sundry aesthetic criticisms, and found its place in the affections of the people of Edinburgh. At the West End the green cupola and golden cross of St. George's West stand out against Corstorphine hill as a landmark for Charlotte Square which still retains at least some of the distinction of Robert Adam's designs. The Square like Princes Street has lost almost all its residential character—but it is one of the most architecturally distinguished sections of office accommodation in the city. In time this photograph may achieve the cachet of a collector's item. The trams which have pitched and rolled and bucketed and trundled their temperamental way along the street for some eighty years, powered by horse and then electricity, have now been relegated to the obscure pastures of redundancy.

Photo: A. F. Kersting

Swanston Cottage

"Long ago this sheltered field was purchased by the Edinburgh magistrates for the sake of the springs that rise or gather there. After they had built their water-house and laid their pipes, it occurred to them that the place was suitable for junketing . . . the dell was turned into a garden; and in the knoll that shelters it from the plain and the sea winds, they built a cottage looking to the hills. They brought crockets and gargoyles from old St. Giles, which they were then restoring, and disposed them on the gables and over the door and about the garden; and the quarry which had supplied them with building material they draped with clematis and carpeted with beds of roses." That, in the words of Robert Louis Stevenson, is an impression of Swanston cottage which his family leased as a holiday home and where he spent many summers as a young man. The hills on to which the house looks are the Pentlands, walked by Stevenson countless times, and remembered eagerly in his later days in Samoa when he knew he would never see them again. In this setting he must have done much of the thinking that diverted his career from the family tradition of lighthouse engineering to the law, and then from the law to writing. Very little has changed at Swanston since Stevenson knew it. The successors of his "purple magistrates" are still the proprietors; the house is still leased to a tenant; the thicket has been thinned out somewhat; a block of brick filter houses has been added to the water scheme: and the hillside has acquired a new population of golfers in the summer and skiers in the winter.

Photo: J. Allan Cash

Pentlands near Glencorse

At the north-eastern end of the Pentlands, Allermuir and Caerketton, the familiars of Robert Louis Stevenson, rise above Swanton. From here the hills run south-west for about sixteen miles through Midlothian and Peeblesshire and taper gradually down into the valley of the Clyde in Lanarkshire. In the main they are modest, domestic hills, the highest summit, Scald Law, standing out at 1898 feet. The range is largely grass-covered and provides good sheep grazing right up to most of the tops. When the building of Edinburgh's New Town demanded an increased water supply the valleys and hollows of the Pentlands were adapted as city reservoirs. Two of Scotland's most notable engineers, Sir John Rennie and Thomas Telford, prepared plans for the Glencorse reservoir which lies behind the ridge of Carnethy Hill, running up to the right of the photograph. The ancient chapel of St. Katherine of the Hopes which was submerged as a result of this operation breaks through the municipal waters occasionally for a brief reappearance in times of severe drought. Further to the south west the moors around Dunsyre and Medwinhead were much used as a centre for Covenanting gatherings, and from this district came the leaders of the rising which ended in defeat by General Tam Dalyell of the Binns at the battle of Rullion Green, fought on the lower slopes of Carnethy. With due respect to civic water schemes and the Covenanting cause, perhaps the greatest interest of the Pentlands lies in their accessibility to the numerous chair-borne citizens of Edinburgh. The wonderful variety of hill walks, within a short bus run of Princes Street, have become a traditional weekend release for the city dwellers and are tramped almost as much in the white of winter as they are in the green and blue of summer and autumn.

Photo: Fred G. Sykes

Forth Bridge and Ferry

Since the regular journeyings of St. Margaret, queen of Malcolm Canmore, in the eleventh century the Queensferry passage has been used as an arterial link between Edinburgh, Fife and the north. The bustling days at the end of last century, when rail fares meant a profit for someone, produced a railway bridge and incidentally an engineering accomplishment which even architects have been known to applaud. But users of the Queen's Highway still make the crossing by ferry as Queen Margaret did nine hundred years ago. The three, great diamond-shaped cantilever sections which won a baronetcy for their designer, Sir John Fowler, make a notable profile in the river view from a surprising assortment of angles in Fife, the Lothians and even Clackmannanshire. For generations their lattice work of steel tubes and girders has offered a challenge to young maiden-voyagers intent on shying a luck-penny from a moving train into the river. The burgh of South Queensferry, which winds west from the bridge, along a narrow main street, has salvaged little more than its name from those early associations with royalty. In the year 1882, when work on the bridge was started, the burgh was struggling out of bankruptcy at a rate of 12s. 6d. in the pound. Its oldest legacy from the past is part of a Carmelite Priory, originally endowed by the local family of Dundas in the early fourteenth century and now in the care of the Scottish Episcopal Church. Across the main street from the priory a seventeenth-century tenement called Plewlands House has survived the various threats and depredations of the years, including a twentieth-century road widening proposal, to have its tenacity rewarded by complete restoration. A mile to the south the tiny Norman church of Dalmeny provides a closer association with the early days of the ferry, when it was operated by the monks of Dunfermline Abbey.

Photo: Fred G. Sykes

Dunfermline Abbey and Palace

The street directory of Dunfermline is an intriguing index to the historic comings and goings in which the town has been involved in the past nine centuries. Close by the precincts of the abbey and the palace are Canmore Street and St. Margaret Street commemorating Malcolm III and his queen who founded, in about 1070, the church of the Holy Trinity from which the abbey grew. In Monastery Street and Priory Lane there is a hint of the great days when the abbey was considered to be one of the most magnificent monastic establishments in Scotland. Bruce Street recalls the burning of the abbey by the English and its eventual reconstruction when King Robert I had regained the throne. Bruce was one of many Kings of Scotland to be buried in the abbey after it superseded Iona as a royal burial place on the death of Malcolm and Margaret. The long and affectionate association of the Royal Stuarts with the palace is remembered in Queen Anne Street and James Street. In the palace James VI's queen, Anne of Denmark, gave birth to a son who became Charles I, and a daughter who became the "Winter Queen" of Bohemia, from whom the present royal family is descended. All that remains of the palace now is a wall of the royal kitchen premises standing between the gardens and the abbey. Kirkgate sums up succinctly the destruction of the abbey in the heat of the Reformation and its subsequent modified repair, for use as a parish church under the name of the Auld Kirk until the New Abbey church rose beside it. And then there is Moodie Street where that latter-day notability Andrew Carnegie was born in humble circumstances. Through Carnegie's bounty Pittencrieff Glen was presented to the town as a public pleasance; its lawns and walks and flower-beds flanking two sides of the ancient abbey and palace.

Photo: A. F. Kersting

St. Monance

There is room for reasonable doubt as to whether the saint after whom this small fishing village in the east neuk of Fife is called was one Monanus from Hungary, who preached the gospel was martyred and enshrined in the neighbourhood, or quite another Moinenn, Bishop of Clonfert, whose relics were brought from Ireland and placed to rest in a church built in his name. At any rate it is clear that there were very early settlements on this spot. Legend has it that King David II was miraculously relieved of a barbed arrow after praying at the shrine of St. Monans and in gratitude founded a new church in 1362—a delightful little building part of which still remains. There is a record that he appointed Sir William Dishington, the Sheriff of Fife, as master-of-works, apparently not so much to design the building as to find funds for the expenses involved. Some of the little houses huddled round the harbour date from the eighteenth and early nineteenth centuries. The red pantiles, which add a jaunty splash of colour to many of the roofs, once came into east coast ports as ballast in ships from the Low Countries trading in salt and coal. Fishing is no longer a staple means of livelihood in St. Monance, although a small fleet operates from the harbour. Like its neighbours on the east neuk, Elie, Pittenweem, Anstruther, Kilrenny and Crail, it has entered the competitive holiday trade and vies with the opposition of Gullane, North Berwick and Dunbar across the Firth of Forth on the coast of East Lothian.

Photo: G. Douglas Bolton

River Isla near Forter

The Isla is one of those Scottish rivers with a dual personality. While it is in Angus its character is predominantly highland, but when it reaches Perthshire it assumes a gentler, lowland aspect. The river starts its course as a burn 3,000 feet up the face of the Glas Maol, little more than a mile from the meeting place of the boundaries of Angus, Perthshire and Aberdeenshire, and comes purling down the Grampian mountainside which rejoices in the shy glories of alpine flowers. Caenlochan just below the Isla's source is one of the few places in Britain where the thistle-like alpine lettuce, with its handsome bearing and large blue flowerheads, is known to grow. In Glenisla the river widens and the landscape opens out a little. There is good farming land here, but it is still untamed enough for that vicious anachronism the wildcat to breed and the blackcock to survive. There are two former strongholds of the Ogilvy family on the banks of the river which were both destroyed within one month by the Earl of Argyll in 1640. Forter Castle at the northern foot of Mount Blair, where a pass runs from Glenisla through to Glenshee, has remained a ruinous shell since Argyll's attack. Further south, after the river has had its final highland fling in the falls of Reekie Linn and the Slug of Auchrannie, it is joined by the Melgam water from the east. Above the meeting of the rivers stood old Airlie Castle protected by water on three sides, but with the master of the house, Lord Airlie, in London to avoid signing the Covenant it was not strong enough to resist Argyll's force. Only a fragment of its rich, red sandstone now exists and it has been replaced by a more modern Airlie Castle, the dower house of the Airlie family. From here the Isla has a more peaceful passage to its meeting with the Tay a few miles north of Stobhall.

Photo: G. Douglas Bolton

Balmoral Castle and Lochnagar

Royal patronage of Deeside, and the wilder mountain country to the south, started when Prince Albert took a forty-year lease of Abergeldie Castle in 1848. Within a few years the neighbouring Forest of Balmoral, to the west, was bought outright by Albert, and later Birkhall to the east was acquired by Edward VII when Prince of Wales. These three estates cover roughly eleven miles along the Dee and stretch south to the granite summit of Lochnagar. The castle of Balmoral, which was designed by an Aberdeen architect in conjunction with Prince Albert, is a nineteenth century variation of the earlier baronial architecture of Aberdeenshire, to be found at Crathes Castle, Craigievar, and Castle Fraser. Queen Victoria and Prince Albert first stayed there in the late summer of 1855, before the building had been quite completed, and since then a summer holiday by the side of the Dee has become firmly, and by all the evidence fondly, established on the royal calendar. Between the castle and the main Deeside road rises a screen of rare conifers and forest trees which makes a contribution to royal privacy and at the same time adds the enhancement of its varied colours to the river scene. When the royal family is not in residence these wooded policies and the castle garden are open to visitors regularly. Overlooking the castle from the top of a small tree-capped hill is a cairn bearing the inscription, "To the beloved memory of Albert the Great and Good, Prince Consort, erected by his broken-hearted widow, Victoria R.— Wisdom of Solomon iv 13, 14."

Photo: G. Douglas Bolton

Macduff Harbour

The shore of the Moray Firth. is yet another stretch of Scottish coastline where holidays have largely supplanted work as a means of livelihood. At Macduff, as at Portsoy, Cullen, Portknockie and the rest, the herring fishing is not what it was. At the turn of the century these harbours were so crowded when the herring fleets came in that it was possible to walk across them stepping from boat to boat. The photograph opposite gives an average impression of the harbour's activity at Macduff today. The town, however, is well endowed for its role as a summer resort. It shares the remarkably dry and sunny climate which favours the counties of Banff, Moray and Nairn, it has an excellent beach, and it is pleasantly planned with the harbour backed by good, plain fisher-town buildings. This plan dates back to the eighteenth century when an Earl of Fife started to develop the small fishing hamlet on the site, known as Doune. As the town grew the old name was changed by James Duff, 2nd Earl of Fife, and it was raised to the status of a burgh of barony. The harbour, which remained a private property of the Duffs until the end of last century, was also improved and as a result it diverted a good deal of trade from its more ancient neighbour at Banff. On the top of Doune hill which climbs away from the harbour stands the auld kirk, clean and seamanlike in a coat of white harl, another contribution to the town by the Earls of Fife.

Photo: A. F. Kersting

Loch Ness

The Great Glen is a whopping geological fault which runs from the Moray Firth, between the mouth of the Findhorn and the Sutors of Cromarty, in a south-westerly direction to the island of Lismore, at the north end of the Sound of Mull. About twenty-four miles of this great crack are taken up with the waters of Loch Ness and further down the glen, connected by the Caledonian Canal, come the lesser lochs of Oich and Lochy and the sea inlet of Loch Linnhe. The geology of the glen is of general interest because it is thought that this fault is a permanent weakness in the earth's crust. At the time of the great Lisbon earthquake in 1755 there was a tremendous disturbance of the waters of Loch Ness producing a series of massive waves which swept along from the Inverness end and flooded the course of the river Oich at its head. The fact of the loch's great depth and its geological peculiarities have been used in more recent times to substantiate some of the many theories propounded on that doughty perennial, the monster of Loch Ness—the loch is so deep, you see . . . never been known to freeze . . . scientific fact . . . prehistoric life . . . possible to survive the Ice Age . . .—But that is too large a question to go into here. It is enough for most visitors that the loch itself should be there with the hills rising from its banks to join the Monadhliath mountains on the east and reaching back into the hydro-electric hinterland of Glen Affric to the west. The wall of red rock exposed by blasting along the road on the north-west shore adds another natural colour to contrast with the greens of the woodlands and the deep blue of the surface of the water.

Canisp and Suilven

The anomaly of Sutherland's name is quickly explained if it is looked upon as the land south of the Orkneys, which it was to the Norsemen who overran it and settled in it during the eleventh century. To the native, present-day Scot this county is very much in the north and generally thought of as a wild combination of bog, loch and unrewarding rock, distinguished by its isolated and individualistic mountains. Certainly the most distinctive of these mountains is Suilven, which seems to be constantly crowding into the view in one of its many forms. Here it is seen from the north-west with the shapely dome of its summit to the fore and its secondary peak coming round the corner. It is rather this view of the mountain which has earned it the name of "sugar-loaf" among the seamen of the Minch. In terms of visual impact Suilven overshadows its taller neighbour Canisp. Seeing Suilven from the southern ridge of Canisp very roughly reverses the view here and brings into the foreground the face of the secondary peak which has a sharper outline than its opposite end, rather like the rear view of a mediaeval knight's helmet and mantling. From the summit of Canisp the sharp ridge of Suilven appears broadside on, with scattered lochs and the Minch beyond, showing to best advantage the plunging sweep of its flanks. It has a lean and alpine look. Like its neighbour Suilven offers rare scope for peak spotting in all directions. There is nothing between it and the islands of Lewis and Harris to the west, to the north the heights of Quinag rise and to the south lies the long ridge of Ben More Coigeach.

Photo: G. Douglas Bolton

Loch Inchard

The Sutherland Clearances, which involved the uprooting of most of the population of the county at the beginning of last century, have survived for more than 150 years as topic of controversy. Depending upon the point of view being put forward the first Duke of Sutherland, who set the clearances in motion, appears either as a bad baron or an enlightened agriculturalist. His problem was to counter-act the recurrent winter famines which afflicted the dispersed crofting communities, and to exploit to better advantage the resources of his lands. The solution he adopted, on expert advice, was to move the crofters to new ground round the coast and to devote the interior to extensive sheep grazing, Compulsory evacuation of independent people even if intended for their own good is bound to raise opposition, but the census figures covering the period of the clearances, with a margin before and after, show that no appreciable depopulation resulted in this case. The shores of Loch Inchard running inland from the North Minch are still comparatively well populated by Sutherland standards. A number of crofts dotted around the head of the loch in the neighbourhood of Rhiconich can be picked out in this photograph. In the gaelic, the barren ground between Loch Inchard and Loch Laxford to the south is known as the 'rough territory' and the stretch to the north of the loch towards Cape Wrath, with its more promising mixture of loam and sand, has earned the name of 'cultivable country.' The solid hump of Arkle, another of Sutherland's solitary mountains, stands up behind Rhiconich and to the left, in this picture, a ridge of Foinaven runs in from the north.

Photo: J. Allan Cash

Quinag

The land between Kylesku, the attractive meeting place of three lochs on the west coast of Sutherland, and Loch Assynt to the south is almost entirely covered by the impressive mass of Quinag. With its companions, Canisp, Suilven and Glasven, Quinag is among the oldest mountains in the British Isles, representing a link with the millions of years of pre-history which geologists take in their stride but which can only be a vague fog to the layman. Tangible evidence of more recent history lies to the south-east of the mountain in a fragment of Ardvreck Castle perched on a rocky peninsula in Loch Assynt. This was the home of Neil Macleod, Laird of Assynt, who found the Marquis of Montrose, lost and starving in the hills, having fled into Sutherland after the defeat of his Royalist army at Culrain in Easter Ross. The great marquis was held prisoner in Ardvreck and then sent south by Macleod to appear before Parliament, and be hung from a gibbet in the High Street of Edinburgh. For his pains Macleod was rewarded by a gift of four hundred bolls of meal. Quite near the castle there are traces of Calda House built about ten years after the Montrose episode by Kenneth Mackenzie, Earl of Seaforth, whose estates at one time stretched the breadth of the country from Kintail in the west to the coast of the north sea in the east. These lands were eventually forfeited by the Seaforths after the '45 Rising and were partly bought by the Earl of Sutherland. Such relics of the grander style of building as Ardvreck and Calda are rarities in Sutherland and come as a surprise among the vast stretches of moor, mountain and water.

Photo: J. Allan Cash

86

Luskentyre Sands, Harris

The main body of the Outer Hebrides runs from the Butt of Lewis in the north, almost on a par with Cape Wrath on the mainland, down through Lewis and Harris which are in fact one island, North Uist, Benbecula, South Uist and Eriskay to Barra in the south. For the most part these islands are bare of trees and comparatively low-lying, with the exception of Harris where Clisham rises to 2622 feet and at least three of its neighbours Ullava, Oreval and Tigra More top the 2,000 foot mark. The boundary between Lewis and Harris follows an irregular line, to the north of these mountains, between the head of Loch Seaforth on the east and Loch Resort on the west. This line is also the county boundary, for Lewis comes within the jurisdiction of Inverness-shire while Harris and the other outer isles are part of Ross and Cromarty. Below the mountains South Harris is tacked on to the rest of the island by a narrow isthmus at Tarbert. The broad golden swathe of the Luskentyre sands lies at the mouth of the river Laxdale south of West Loch Tarbert looking out to the island of Taransay off-shore. Further down the coast there is a broad beach of similar sand between the little village of Northton and the Toe of Harris sticking out into the Atlantic. Most of the population of Harris is concentrated in the southern half of the island, finding their livelihood in a combination of crofting, fishing and weaving tweed. Midway between Northton and Rodil the little port of Obbe retains its more recent name of Leverburgh as an epitaph from the time of Lord Leverhulme's abortive attempt to elevate the fisheries and agriculture on the island to the level of big business.

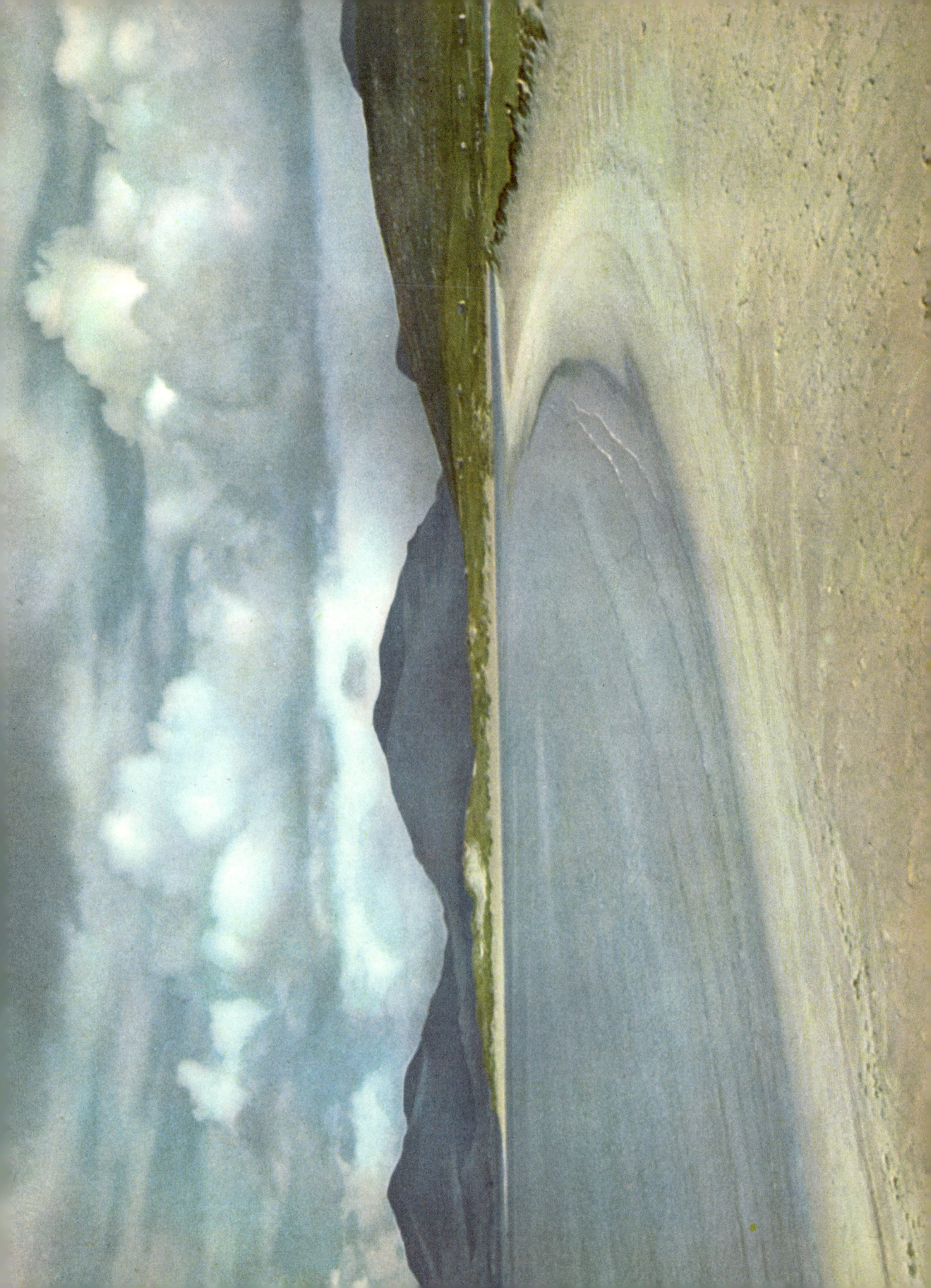

In the Cuillins, Skye

The central mountain mass of Skye divides itself naturally into two clearly defined groups completely dissimilar in colour and contour. Back from the stretch of coast between Broadford and Loch Sligachan, which looks on to the island of Scalpay, the Red Hills stand in orderly assembly. They tend towards a regular shape, their steep slopes streaked with crumbling, red granite scree rising to rounded summits. Across Glen Sligachan to the south-west the character of the mountains changes and the craggy tops of the Cuillins come into their own. The main peaks are Sgurr nan Gillean, Sgurr a Chreadaidh, Sgurr Alasdair, and Sgurr nan Eag; all of hard, black volcanic rock and linked together in one tortuous, precipitous ridge with Loch Coruisk lying at its heart. In this photograph taken from the lower slopes of Sgurr nan Gillean, looking over Glen Sligachan, the dramatic profile of Blaven is outlined against the clouds. This mountain is something of an in-between. In character it is one of the Cuillins but it is divorced from the main chain and stands nearer the Red Hills. The summit of Sgurr nan Gillean is one of the finest in the group. Its buttressed pinnacles, where snow lies late on the north faces, crowding in behind each other as if thrusting upwards in an effort for maximum height. One look at these crags from a distance should be enough to convince anyone that they are not meat for the inexperienced climber, but perhaps it is worth emphasising that they are positively dangerous without skilled company. The saving consolation is that there is no dearth of knowledgable climbers eager to add numbers to the brotherhood, and the Cuillins make an incomparable setting for acquiring experience.

Photo: J. Allan Cash

Dunvegan Castle

Dunvegan on its rocky base at the head of Loch Dunvegan to the north-west of Skye has been the home of the Macleods of Macleod for seven and a half centuries. A fair variety of castellated architecture has gone into the development of the building in the course of all these years, and it makes an interesting subject for analysis. In the beginning there was most probably a very simple form of stronghold and courtyard enclosed by a thick retaining wall, like that seen springing from the rock in this photograph with a doorway near its base. That doorway, in fact, does carry grooves for a portcullis. The square keep to the left is thought to be an addition of the fourteenth century, and includes, under the high tower which is a later embellishment, the old guardroom and a bottle-shaped dungeon. Behind the projecting wing on the right a chimney head marks the north-east tower attributed to Alastair Crotach —Crookback—Macleod, who died in 1528 and was buried in the delightful church of St. Clement's at Rodil across the Little Minch on the southern tip of the island of Harris. Joining the keep and Alastair Crotach's tower is a central range dating from the time of Rory More, a notable Macleod chief who was knighted by James VI for maintaining a semblance of law and order in the west highlands. Another legacy from Rory More which survives at Dunvegan is his drinking horn, capacity about two quarts, which the heir of the Macleods traditionally drains at one go before succeeding to the chieftainship. In recent years the enormous task of completely restoring Dunvegan has been going ahead steadily under the supervision of Dame Flora Macleod of Macleod, head of the clan.

Photo: J. Allan Cash

Loch Maree

From almost any conceivable angle the setting of Loch Maree is magnificent. Here at the foot of the loch, in the region of Tollie, where it starts to drain into the sea waters of Loch Ewe the prospect is from low ground looking up to the ridges and peaks of Ben Airidh Charr. Approaching the head of the loch, on the other hand, through Glen Docherty a twist in the road suddenly throws the whole fiord-like vista of blue water and flanking mountains into view below, with the massive grey shapes of Ben Eighe and Slioch standing by on left and right. Coming out of the glen at loch level the road runs into the little village of Kinlochewe—head of Loch Ewe—a name that argues a case for the theory that Loch Maree and Loch Ewe were at one time all of a piece and that silting action has caused the difference in levels of thirty odd feet which now separates them. About five miles beyond the village Glen Grudie offers the chance of a "backdoor" view of Ben Eighe, and across the loch Ben Lair competes gracefully with its heftier neighbour Slioch. The dense greens of Forestry Commission conifer plantations sweep down to the loch-side at Slattadale and contrast with the natural growth on the group of islands off-shore. A small boy called Osgood Mackenzie who cut the first sod of the Loch Maree road, when it was started as a relief measure during the great famine in the middle of the last century, created later in life the extraordinary highland garden of Inverewe which lies round the corner from Tollie on a small peninsula jutting into Loch Ewe. Here, in the midst of this wild country, rhododendrons, azaleas, tree ferns, eucalyptus, palms, magnolias and all manner of exotics flourish in a bewildering succession of colour that lasts almost the year round.

Photo: J. Allan Cash

An Teallach from above Gruinard Hill

The red Torridonian sandstone which has been exposed with colourful effect in the creation of rock gardens at Inverewe is more massively represented in the towering ridges of An Teallach to the north-east. Bidein a' Ghlas Thuill, the summit of the mountain, reaches a height of 3,483 feet and Sgurr Fiona, the second peak, has been sculptured by the wind and the weather into a series of terraced precipices which hold the winter snows well into the summer. Above the ascending cliffs of Sgurr Fiona rides a serrated crest of pinnacles and pyramids which is probably the nearest likeness to the tops of the Cuillins of Skye to be found on the mainland. Between the mountain and the deep waters of the North Minch lies Gruinard Bay into which the Little Gruinard river flows from the outlet of the Fionn Loch high up behind Ben Airidh Charr. The river meets the bay at a small cove dressed with fine, bleached sands and surrounded by knobbly moraine which still retains something of the polish imparted by glaciers of the Ice Age. A mile and a bit to the north the Gruinard river, big brother of the Little Gruinard, finds its way into the bay below Gruinard House having started out from the foot of Loch na Sheallag at the base of An Teallach. Looking to the north over the bay, from the viewpoint of this photograph, the Summer Isles lie scattered in the outer mouth of Loch Broom, and in the distance the lonely shapes of Canisp and Suilven rise to mark the beginnings of Sutherland.

Photo: G. Douglas Bolton

Loch Broom

The mouth of Loch Broom takes a great bite out of the coast line in the northern corner of Wester Ross, including the Summer Isles in its sweep. Inland it divides into Loch Broom proper to the north, and Little Loch Broom and Gruinard Bay to the south. Overlooking this line of division from the north are the long ridges of Ben More Coigeach, a striking mountain which offers wonderful variety of colour and outline. Two hill lochs to the south provide the head waters for Loch Broom. Up the Dirrie More, Loch Droma releases a river of the same name, and the Cuileig runs out of Loch A Bhraoin at the base of A' Chailleach, one of the Fannich peaks, to meet it in the strath below Braemore. Of the two the Droma has the more thrilling run. By the junction of the Ullapool and Dundonnell roads it cascades over the Falls of Measach dropping 200 feet into the spectacular narrow canyon of Corrieshalloch Gorge. The road which turns off near the falls for Dundonnell and Little Loch Broom retains the name of Destitution Road from its origin in the need to find work for local people during the famine of the mid-nineteenth century. Along the eastern shore of Loch Broom, which carries the main road to Ullapool, a succession of rocky promontories break out into the water, and here and there patches of woodland add splashes of colour to the hillside. As with all west highland lochs, however, it is the blending of water and mountain background in the ceaselessly changing light which is the real core of its attraction.

Photo: J. Allan Cash

Ullapool

It seems a far cry from the American War of Independence to the evening quiet of Shore Street and the waters of Loch Broom at Ullapool, but history in its devious way has worked them both into the same pattern. The colonists' victory not only punctured Britain's prestige but produced a strong feeling of resentment at the poor dividends shown on a considerable investment of time and money. An indirect result of this was the search for new, and safer, outlets for the colonising urge which had its roots well set in the British system. New surveys of the Highlands indicated good prospects, and there were also men of goodwill who thought something should be done to benefit the northerly parts of the country. It was in these circumstances that the British Fisheries Society was founded and set out to establish a fishing station and town at Ullapool in 1788. The simple and attractive white-washed houses all have the stamp of good design that distinguishes the domestic building of the late eighteenth and early nineteenth centuries in Scotland. Undoubtedly too, they owe something to the influence of two outstanding designers of the time. Both Robert Mylne, the architect, and Thomas Telford, the bridge builder and engineer, were commissioned by the Fisheries Society to advise on the development of the town. These little houses have survived a failure in the herring fishing, which put the Society out of business in Ullapool seventy years after it moved in; they have remained to see the fishing pick up again to some degree; and they now welcome each year the kind of fishing society that pursues salmon and sea trout in preference to the simple herring.

Photo: G. Douglas Bolton

Glenshiel

Narrowly confined between mountains of the 3,000 feet class Glenshiel lies deep in the old domain of the Mackenzies of Kintail. To the north-east it is bounded by the steep grassy slopes of the Five Sisters of Kintail, with Scour Ouran, the peak of the well, standing out as the highest summit, and to the south-west by the sprawling shape of the Saddle. This is wonderful hill-walking country, uncomplicated by discouraging rock faces and yet offering the exhilaration of maintaining a height between 2,500 and 3,000 feet along extensive ridges. The Mackenzies of Kintail, Earls of Seaforth, were strong supporters of the Jacobite cause in the first half of the eighteenth century and fought one minor skirmish on their home ground in Glenshiel, under the shoulder of Sgurr na Ciste Dubh, in 1719. After putting up slight resistance to a Hanoverian army the Jacobites, including a detachment of Spanish troops, took to the hills and dispersed. In very short time the Spaniards were taken prisoner in a mountain gully which has been known ever since as the Corrie of the Spaniards. It is an interesting commentary on clan loyalties that even when the Earl of Seaforth forfeited his estates and went into exile his factor in this area continued to collect his rents and send them on to the Continent, instead of to the Government committee of estates. The head of Glenshiel marks the line of the watershed of Scotland. Here the Cluanie and the Shiel rise within half a mile of each other; the first to find its way out into the Moray firth by Loch Cluanie, Glen Moriston and Loch Ness, and the Shiel to head for the Atlantic by way of Loch Duich and Loch Alsh.

Photo: J. Allan Cash

Loch Duich

The rock of Eilean Donan, south of Dornie where the mouth of Loch Duich meets the waters of Loch Long and Loch Alsh, was looked upon as a commanding situation in earlier times. It is thought that it was once the site of an ancient Caledonian fort, and certainly there has been a stronghold of some kind on it since the early thirteenth century. In the fifteenth and sixteenth centuries it was a castle of the Mackenzies of Kintail, and later in this capacity made a brief appearance in the prelude to the battle of Glenshiel. Lord Seaforth's Spanish contingent garrisoned the castle but were forced to retreat almost immediately by three English warships which demolished the building with broadsides from the loch. As seen today it is a twentieth century re-build, and the home of one of the Macrae family who were once comrades-in-arms of the Mackenzies. Loch Duich runs inland behind the castle towards the Five Sisters of Kintail which can be seen rising in the background above the attractively arched gangway linking Eilean Donan to the mainland. Progressing up the loch the Sisters change face constantly until, near the head, the five peaks display their separate features in a towering skyline. Morvich at the head of the loch is the start of one route leading to the hills behind Kintail which harbour in their isolation the highest waterfall in Great Britain. The Glomach burn comes out of Loch a' Bhealaich under the heights of Ben Attow and flows north to its narrow plunge over the falls which it accomplishes in two atomising drops; one of 300 feet, followed by a bounce of 50 feet from a projecting rock. From the pool at the foot of the falls the burn continues to meet the Elchaig and runs west with it to the head of Loch Long.

Photo: A. F. Kersting

White Sands of Morar

The tentative beginnings of the '45 Rising, when Prince Charles Edward Stuart had to exert all his powers of charm and coercion to win the support of his Highland chiefs, and the final surrender of the Stuart cause were both enacted in the Morar district. Prince Charles landed at Borrodale on the shore of Loch nan Uamh in 1745 prior to raising his standard inland at the head of Loch Shiel, and fourteen months later, defeated and hunted, he came off the Braes of Morar to embark at the same spot on a French privateer, inappropriately named *L'Heureux*. North of Borrodale the district is divided by the tremendous depth of Loch Morar, which is reckoned at more than 1,000 feet and considered to be the deepest known hollow in Europe with the exception of a submarine valley skirting the south of Scandinavia. A short river with a good reputation for salmon fishing crosses the narrow clasp of land at the foot of the loch and carries its overflow down to the sea. Spreading outwards from the river's mouth along the shore of a small sea loch are the white sands of Morar, made up from pulverised fragments of a coral-like, reef-building alga washed up by the tide. In early summer carpets of marsh marigolds and wild hyacinths, and patches of yellow flag irises, bloom in profusion above the high water mark, and local gardens are filled with the glorious colours of azaleas. Over the Sound of Sleat, to the south-west the plateau of the Isle of Eigg fills the view and in this photograph a southerly shoulder of Rum intrudes on the extreme right.

Photo: Fred G. Sykes

Ben Nevis seen from Corpach

Confronted with Ben Nevis face to face, as in this view from Corpach looking over Fort William, there is no doubt that it is a mountain of consequence, but the lack of a distinctive peak almost denies its full stature as the highest mountain in Great Britain (4,406 ft). The one sure way to put qualms of uncertainty at rest is to climb to the summit, from where it is immediately obvious that everything else within the range of vision is being looked down on. This ascent can be comparatively easy or difficult according to taste. Normally the route taken is the road up Glen Nevis which climbs the western slopes for about two miles and then joins a pony track bearing left to continue to the summit. If the top is without its all too frequent mantle of cloud a possible, but hardly probable, view would include the Mamores to the south, and the peaks of Glencoe immediately beyond, Ben More on Mull, the Paps of Jura, and Ben Cruachan; to the south-east Ben Vorlich on Loch Lomond, Ben More behind Glen Dochart, Ben Lawers on Loch Tay, and that recurring landmark Schiehallion above the head of Loch Rannoch; Scour Ouran to the north-west, and further west again, the Cuillins. All these are worth looking for but they are not likely to be bagged in one day. From Corpach the last sinuous lap of the road to the isles runs west in company with a branch of the West Highland Railway line along the shores of Loch Eil and past Glenfinnan towards Mallaig and the ferry to Skye.

Photo: A. F. Kersting

Loch Leven and the Peaks of Glencoe

Reading from left to right across this photograph the mountains of Glencoe start with Sgurr na Ciche more commonly known as the Pap of Glencoe, and the fissured face of Sgurr nan Fiannaidh, both of which lie on the north of the glen. Then comes Meall Mor to the south with the snow covered peak of Stob Coire nan Lochan and the true summit of Bidean nam Bian rising behind. Lying dark on the water in front of the Pap is the small Eilan Munde where MacIan, chief of the Macdonalds, was buried after being shot during the massacre of 1692. The face of Meall Mor carries the scar of the Ballachulish slate quarries, once a thriving industry supplying durable, dark blue slates throughout the country, but now more or less abandoned after a series of failures and revivals. Striking through the glen, beyond Meall Mor, four outlying spurs of Bidean are the main features; first Ant Sron and then the Three Sisters, Aonach Dubh, Gearr Aonach and Beinn Fhada, overlaid with a thin veneer of tufted grass and moss which gives way to bare rock as the height increases. Across the river Coe the great notched ridge of Aonach Eagach runs east from Sgurr nan Fiannaidh to make a northern boundary. It is a matter of opinion whether or not this ridge is a better test of the hill-walker's nerve than the Cir Mhor crest on Arran. The glen finally breaks out into the open at its eastern end past the two shepherds of Etive, Buachaille Etive Beag and Buachaille Etive Mor, the latter standing out like a vast pyramid when seen on the approach over the Moor of Rannoch. More than 12,000 acres of the glen are now protected from despoliation and are freely accessible to the public, under the ownership of the National Trust for Scotland.

Photo: G. Douglas Bolton